W9-BWG-809

"GENTLEMEN, MORE DOLCE PLEASE!"

"GENTLEMEN, MORE DOLCE PLEASE!"

An Irreverent Memoir of Thirty Years in the Boston Symphony Orchestra

By HARRY ELLIS DICKSON

Beacon Press Boston

Library of Congress catalog card number: 70–84793
Beacon Press books are published under the auspices
of the Unitarian Universalist Association

Printed in the United States of America

The photographs in this book are reproduced
by courtesy of the Boston Symphony Orchestra

TO MY WIFE, JANE—who advised against it

PREFACE

A musician's life is different from that of most people. We don't go to an office every day, or to a factory, or a bank. We go to an empty hall. We don't deal in anything tangible, nor do we produce anything except sounds. We saw away, or blow, or pound for a few hours and then we go home. It is a strange way to make a living! No wonder my neighbor once asked, "How do you really earn your livelihood?" This book is my reply.

For thirty years I have kept a chronicle of events in the Boston Symphony. Some of them were painfully unfunny at the time, yet now they bring back pleasant memories.

As a musician and as a Bostonian I am fiercely proud of the Boston Symphony Orchestra, and I am grateful for being a part of it. During my conservatory years it was my ambition to join the orchestra. It may sound maudlin now, but as a student I used to tip my hat whenever I passed Symphony Hall. And now after thirty years of membership in the orchestra I am still grateful, because no other life could have given me such rich and rewarding experiences. So, once again I doff my hat to the Boston Symphony Orchestra, its present, past, and future members. Long may it sing—ever more *dolce!*

ACKNOWLEDGMENT

For five years I gave weekly pre-symphony talks at the luncheons before the Friday concerts of the Boston Symphony and found, to my amazement, that my audience was more than casually interested in us as people. As a result of these talks I was tempted to write this book, but nothing would have come of my temptation without the urging and encouragement of my good friend, Professor David Manning White, Chairman of the Division of Journalism at Boston University. An incurable music lover, he has been a patient and persistent midwife. And if the baby is less than a prodigy, it is through no fault of his. His work was done faithfully and courageously—considering the man he had to work with.

I am also indebted to Mrs. Serge Koussevitzky for permission to publish twelve of her drawings in this book.

CONTENTS

"GENTLEMEN, MORE DOLCE PLEASE!"

THE MUSICIANS

Every orchestra musician has a pet frustration and each would like to be something or somebody else. One evening before a string-quartet concert our former solo violist, the late Jean LeFranc, was furiously pacing up and down the greenroom practicing and muttering to himself. "You know, Dickson," he said to me, "I have played perhaps five, six thousand concerts in my life. All the time I am nervous. Better to be a plumbair!"

Each musician is deeply concerned with his own technical problems, and each envies the others. There is probably not one oboe player in the whole world who is satisfied with his lot, not a horn player who doesn't look forward eagerly to his retirement, not a string player who wouldn't rather play one of the "easy" wind instruments, and so on throughout the orchestra. But . . .

After many years of close observation it seems clear that, with few exceptions, certain characteristics go with certain instruments. Whether these characteristics prompted the choice of instrument or were acquired because of the instrument I don't know. But they are there for all to notice.

For instance, the cellists are the greatest source of trouble in an orchestra. They are the prima donnas, supersensitive, suspicious, conceited, quarrelsome, and altogether a pain in the neck to themselves, the conductor, and the rest of the orchestra.

Among the dozen cellists in an orchestra if you find two who speak to each other, things are going quite well. Most of all they hate bass players, and when Serge Koussevitzky first came to the Boston Symphony Orchestra as our conductor with his reputation as a former bass virtuoso, the cellists of the orchestra looked upon him with a certain amount of disdain. After all, Arturo Toscanini was a cellist, and so was Sir John Barbirolli, and they were conductors—but a bass player? Shortly after his appointment, Koussevitzky was asked by the basses of the orchestra to play for the men. After some hesitation and a bit of coaxing, he did play for them, and one of the cellists later reported to his wife, "It was astounding! I never heard such bass playing. I closed my eyes and said to myself, 'That is not a bass. It sounds like a lousy cello!'"

There was a time when the basses were the solid citizens of an orchestra. They did their job, giving no trouble and expecting no praise. But Koussevitzky changed all that. Throughout the world now bass players have become almost as prima-donna-ish, cantankerous, and pugnacious as cellists.

Viola players in an orchestra are usually the least troublesome. They are mostly ex-fiddlers who have become philosophical about their role of playing, especially in classical music, the deadly, dull inner voice. A story is told about a viola player who dreamed he was playing Handel's "Messiah," and woke up to find he was! Most viola players smoke a pipe and look with detached humor upon the foibles of their colleagues. They don't even resent it when they are looked upon by their violinist colleagues as broken-down fiddlers. There was a time when the viola section of an orchestra was made up of the oldest men and any player under sixty would be looked upon with great sympathy. "So young, and already viola!" But with modern demands upon the violist his capabilities now must be on a par with a violinist.

The violins in an orchestra are divided into two sections, firsts and seconds. They both play the same instruments, yet what a difference in status between the two! And this is so completely wrong, because in a good orchestra there is no dif-

The Boston Symphony Orchestra under Erich Leinsdorf.
Photograph by Photography Incorporated.

ference in the abilities of the players. A man starts as a second violinist, then eventually moves into the firsts, depending on the longevity of the latter. Yet in the mind of the public there is a kind of stigma against "playing second fiddle." In reality the second-violin part is just as important to a composition as any other. (Years ago I overheard the end of an argument between a German triangle player and another colleague: "Mine part is just so prominenten like your'n!") Some day, I hope, we will do away with the term "second violin." Perhaps "mezzo-violin" would be better. It is possible that in the future the term will disappear altogether, as composers like Stravinsky and others have begun to write for the entire massed violins as a unit. But until this practice becomes universal the first violins in the orchestra will continue to be the aristocrats, emitting an aura of superiority no matter how undeserved, while the seconds remain frustrated and unsung.

Among the woodwinds one immediately focuses on the untouchable oboe players. If they are slightly less troublesome than the cellists, it is only because there are fewer of them. Oboe players are a breed unto themselves. They are the unhappiest of musicians, constantly complaining and bemoaning their fate at having to play such an unpredictable, treacherous instrument. They know nothing about music. They don't have time to learn! Most of their time is spent on shaving their double-reeds. The typical picture of an oboe player, on and off the stage, is one with oboe resting in lap while, with his trusty scalpel, he furiously fashions his reed. From time to time he will attach the reed to the instrument, put it to his pursed lips and blow. Then the inevitable look of dissatisfaction, the removal of the reed, and the return to more shaving. On the stage the oboist is the most detached member of the orchestra—and the most fidgety. The next time you go to a concert watch the oboe section. There is constant activity, completely unrelated to the music. Each time there is more than a bar rest the reed is removed, inspected, cursed, then put back just in time for the next entrance. Between movements the reed is shaved with the trusty knife that lies next to every oboe player. While the music is going on, the oboists confer with one another, thump their instruments, blow through the keys with a hissing sound to remove the water, and generally behave as though there were no concert. And they couldn't care less! To the first-class oboist the over-all continuity of a composition means nothing. His world consists of turning out musical phrases, in tune, in rhythm, and with good sound. The rest is not his concern.

The first oboist of every orchestra is usually not on speaking terms with the conductor, and he hates string players with a passion. He gives his "A" to the orchestra a quarter tone flat, convinced that in a short time they will sabotage him by playing sharp anyway. For some reason all first oboists are gangsters.

They are tough, irascible, double-reed roosters, feared by their colleagues and most conductors. Yet, some of my best friends. . . .

The dandies of any orchestra are the flute players, the best-dressed, the quietest, the most gentlemanly, and the easiest to get along with. They play the least troublesome of all instruments—no reed trouble, no mouthpiece trouble, no string trouble—and so usually they are the best adjusted citizens of a symphony orchestra. And usually the most affluent. Everybody wants to take flute lessons.

Clarinetists are the classic cry-babies of every orchestra. They play a single-reed instrument and look down their noses at any kind of vibrato, making it very difficult for them to play in tune (which they don't) or to adjust to the other choirs. They are forever hunting for a good reed, which they never find, and are constantly being persecuted, they think, by the conductor.

Bassoon players are hobbyists, a most affable lot. They too, like the oboists, play a double-reed instrument, but evidently it affects them differently. The bassoonist is as sweet as the oboist is sour. With his myriad outside activities—telescope-making, flying, bow-making, organ-building—every bassoon player is a handyman. And usually highly intelligent. Why, I don't know. Someone should make a scientific study.

Now for the brass. First the trumpets. Most trumpet players are handsome, debonair, and dashing. And even when they grow old and gray, they retain a certain air of charm. They are usually *bons vivants* with a taste for good wines and pretty women. Most trumpet players are bachelors—or should be.

Trombone players are very much like ministers. Usually quiet, dull, and very moral, they are the good, solid citizens of an orchestra, never complaining, going about their business quietly and efficiently. Nobody ever heard of a rebellious trombone player. If one does begin to feel some stirring of rebellion within himself, he usually quits or becomes personnel manager.

If trombonists are ministerial, horn players certainly are not. They are the rebels of the brass section. As a matter of fact they are the rebels of the orchestra, and conductors are usually afraid of them. The most dissatisfied of all the musicians, constantly agitating for more pay and less work, horn players have been able to convince conductors that their lips can only stand so much (or so little!) playing, and most symphony orchestras have double platoons. It is practically unheard of that one horn player should play an entire concert! The horn is admittedly a treacherously difficult instrument, one of the reasons being that the player can never develop enough stamina to practice sufficiently to master the instrument. Perhaps that is why horn players usually drink a lot.

Before we leave the brasses let us dwell for a moment upon the lowly and lonely tuba player. There is only one in the entire orchestra and he enjoys a certain amount of prestige—and loneliness. Tuba players never talk. They are silent, morose, uncommunicative, but they sing to themselves. They have no common interests with any of their colleagues and, as a matter of fact, most tuba players feel that they don't even belong in the orchestra. They usually strike up a strong friendship with the stage manager. How does one get to be a tuba player? Most became so by accident; someone willed a tuba to the family, the local town band needed one, etc., etc. Nevertheless, the present-day tuba player in a symphony orchestra is an artist in his craft. The young man recently engaged by the B.S.O. does the most amazing things on his unwieldy instrument, including playing all the French horn concertos, for which he has not endeared himself to his horn colleagues.

The percussion players are the strong, virile he-men of any orchestra, and if we were ever threatened physically, they would be our front-line defenses. Since percussionists play many instruments, they are Jacks-of-all-trades, constantly fixing and building, and they can repair anything from a tambourine to a violin to an automobile.

The tympanist is the grand potentate of the percussionists and he almost never deigns to play anything but his soup-kettles. During a performance, while his underlings scurry back and forth from triangle to snare to block to xylophone to cymbal, he presides quietly and benignly over his pigskins, gavel in each hand, proudly surveying his domain.

Finally, we come to a breed apart, the male harpist. He is the Beau Brummell of the orchestra. He plays so seldom that he has plenty of time to shop for new clothes, with the result that he is often taken, by strangers, to be the conductor. He is always well-shaved, well-dressed, and beautifully manicured.

If musicians have mental and emotional characteristics that go with their instruments, they also have readily identifiable physical scars. If the dead body of any musician were found, a little detective work would reveal the instrument he played. For instance, the calluses on the fingers of the left hand mark every string player. The violinist would also have a mark under his left chin, the viola player a slightly larger mark. A cellist could be identified by his left-hand calluses plus one on his left thumb, for he is the only string player who uses that thumb, and a red mark on his chest, the result of pressing the cello toward him. A string-bass player would have much larger hands and larger calluses, and the jazz musician would, in addition, have calluses on his right hand, the result of constantly slapping the strings.

But what about left-handed violinists? I know of only two, although there must be others. Rudolph Kolisch, founder of the Kolisch String Quartet, now teaching at the New England Conservatory of Music in Boston, is a fine violinist who, because of an accident to two fingers of his left hand, learned to play holding the violin in his right hand. The other left-handed violinist is Charlie Chaplin—and why he plays that way I don't know. Actually, even if a person is left-handed, he can learn to play the violin normally, because at the beginning he is equally awkward with either hand. Our concertmaster of the Boston Symphony, Joseph Silverstein, happens to be left-handed, yet he plays "right-handed."

Every clarinetist has, on the inside of his left thumb, his own brand of callus, the result of years of supporting his instrument upon it. The unmistakable battle scars of the harpist are the calluses on only eight fingers. The little fingers are never used in playing the harp; that is, they are never used by professional harpists. The one exception was the late Harpo Marx, who was largely self-taught. He once came to Bernard Zighera, our distinguished harpist, for a lesson, and Zighera was so flabbergasted at the completely unorthodox way in which Marx played, and played well, that he told him he couldn't teach him anything! Besides, Marx was earning more money than Zighera.

Double-reed players, like oboists and bassoonists, could easily be identified by the raw irritation on the inside of their lips, the result of constant pressure against the teeth, and brass players all have elongated upper lips.

Actually it is a small miracle that we don't have a knock-down and drag-out fight among ourselves now and then, particularly after a grueling rehearsal when the conductor (who, too, has feet of clay and may have fought with his wife at breakfast) has been riding the orchestra pretty hard. But there is a charisma about being in Boston and in the Boston Symphony that never allows for such indignities. To be sure, there are some who don't talk to one another, but it is of no consequence. String players may profess to hate oboe players, and clarinetists may proclaim undying hatred toward horn players, and cellists may go on despising each other forever, yet when the conductor gives the downbeat, there is a mysterious inner-communication among all the players, feelings are submerged, and through some minor miracle there is a concerted effort to make music. Afterwards, they may all go back to hating each other! Yet, not too seriously, for the very nature of our profession tends to soften the human heart. And we do have other interests.

Would anyone ever imagine that two of our violinists were former amateur boxers? Or that another is an expert auto mechanic? Or another a former competitive speed-skater? Bassoonist Ernst Panenka, Viennese by birth, is an amateur astronomer who spent years building his own telescope, and now, on moonlit nights when we are not playing, he invites his colleagues to his roof to study the stars. His colleague, bassoonist Sherman Walt, is an ex-fighter pilot of World War II whose present hobby is skiing. We have three licensed pilots in the orchestra, Bill Waterhouse, Joe Hearne, and Bill Stokking, all of whom fly their own planes. Sheldon Rotenberg, violinist and former captain in Intelligence in World War II, is an expert tennis player, having coached the tennis team of his alma mater, Tufts University. Burton Fine, our first violist, holds a couple of college degrees and was formerly employed by N.A.S.A. in the development of our space program. Bob Karol, violist, and Jimmie Stagliano, first horn, are expert golfers who regularly shoot in the seventies.

Martin Hoherman, assistant first cellist, came to the United States from his native Poland by way of Singapore and Hong Kong after a stint in the British Army. In addition to his great abilities as an outstanding cellist, he plays nine or ten other instruments and is occasionally called upon to perform when needed, as pianist, banjoist, saxophonist, or what have you. Name the instrument, Martin Hoherman will play it. And if he can't, give him a few hours' practice time. He also repairs watches.

Karl Zeise, another of our fine cellists, is an art expert and amateur painter who arranges the Symphony Hall exhibits in the art gallery. Pat Cardillo, clarinetist, is the great chef of the Boston Symphony. His culinary skills are such that an invitation to one of his meals is eagerly sought by all his colleagues. There used to be a fierce rivalry between him and Joe dePasquale, and for years I received free meals by acting as referee. I would be invited to one house, and then the other, and pronounce each meal better than anything the other had ever cooked!

Bassoonist Matthew Ruggiero repairs violins and rehairs bows. What started as a hobby has now turned into a substantial side occupation for him and a great convenience for all the string players in the orchestra. Richard Plaster, our contrabassoonist, builds organs and clavichords in his spare time. Charles Yancich, our associate first French horn player, lives in the country and raises golden retrievers. Everett Firth, tympanist, is an art collector and has a sizable collection of American nineteenth and twentieth century paintings in his own art gallery. Vincent Mauricci, viola player, buys and sells real estate, while cellist Mischa Nieland is the stock-market expert.

Violist Reuben Green is an expert ceramicist who has exhibited many of his fine pieces. One would think that dangerous tools would be taboo for a musician, yet violinist Noah Bielski, who played in Carnegie Hall at the age of seven, now spends his spare time in his home workshop, surrounded by various woodworking tools, including a set of electric saws.

But perhaps the most unusual second interest in the orchestra is that of Bill Marshall, who sits on the first stand of second violins. The Reverend William Marshall was recently ordained a Pentecostal minister, and I doubt that any other orchestra in the world can claim a member of the clergy among its personnel.

Ours is a good life in the Boston Symphony. It is hard, exacting, emotional, yet stimulating and rewarding. Musicians gripe constantly (and thank God for the gripers, who bring eventual benefits to all!), yet almost no one ever wants to leave. Players keep staying "one more year" until, in some cases, they are nearly eighty. Of course there are the inevitable exceptions. We had a bassoon player who retired in his middle fifties. He was a marvelous player who claimed he hated music and when he left the orchestra, he vowed he would never touch the instrument again except to plant flowers in it—which he did. There was also a horn player whose ambition was to throw his horn under the wheels of Koussevitzky's car and calmly walk off to his retirement. I once overheard the following conversation between two Russian violinists. "Nicolai, I vould like to retire. Vot should I do?" "Just play for the conductor!"

Playing in the Boston Symphony is generally a lifetime affair. Hardly anyone ever leaves the orchestra until he is ready to retire. In the past few years, however, there have been some notable exceptions. Our first violist, Joseph dePasquale, was tempted with a very substantial financial offer to go to his native Philadelphia, where he now not only plays in that orchestra, but also teaches at his alma mater, the Curtis Institute of Music. He also has three brothers in the Philadelphia Orchestra—two violinists and a cellist—and together they form a unique brothers' quartet.

To Bostonians the leaving of dePasquale, and also our first cellist, Samuel Mayes, was shocking, especially since they left to go to the Philadelphia Orchestra, which everyone knows is *not* the Boston Symphony! Why did they leave? Perhaps they were overcome by the Hungarian charm of Ormandy.

The Boston Symphony personnel generally remains stable. Whatever changes take place do so mostly among the mercurial cellists. In the past few years two have left the orchestra for professional teaching positions and three have left to take solo positions in other orchestras.

The majority of players in the B.S.O. stay throughout their full careers, which extends in some cases to a ripe old age. One of our violinists, Sam Diamond, recently went home after an evening rehearsal and died peacefully in his sleep, after fifty years with the orchestra.

We have no mandatory retirement age in the Boston Symphony. William Kincaide, one of the great flutists of our time, was retired from the Philadelphia Orchestra while still playing beautifully, only because he had reached their retirement age of sixty-five. John Corigliano, admirable concertmaster of the New York Philharmonic, also had to leave when he reached sixty-five (a very young and still enormously capable sixty-five), only to be welcomed as concertmaster in another orchestra.

The question has been raised that if players can be forcibly retired at sixty-five, why not conductors?

An orchestra tends to stabilize itself at various player age-levels over the years. When I joined the orchestra as one of its youngest members, the average age of the players was a good deal higher than it is today. Most have gradually retired, so that today our average age is much lower; and this means that our present personnel will remain substantially the same for many years to come. We do not anticipate many changes in the foreseeable future. Indeed, as one Back Bay dowager said, "Why should anyone leave Boston? After all, we are *here!*"

SYMPHONY HALL—TEMPLE OF MUSIC

Serge Koussevitzky always referred to Symphony Hall as "our temple," and indeed this wonderful hall has been, since 1900, the mecca of musical activity in and around Boston. No matter that occasionally it has been the scene of nonmusical affairs, like commencement exercises, political rallies, banquets, and even New Year parties; it still remains a respected house of things artistic. The fact that Symphony Hall in Boston is one of the most perfect acoustical auditoriums in the world is no accident. It was the first concert hall ever to be built in known conformity with scientific acoustical laws, and to Professor Wallace C. Sabine, then assistant professor of physics at Harvard, goes the credit for this achievement; also to the architects of the hall, McKim, Meade, and White, for their integrity in following his specifications. Would that all subsequent architects of concert halls had displayed the same kind of selfless integrity!

Symphony Hall seats 2,631 people for regular concerts, 2,345 when the floor seats are removed and tables installed for the Pops concerts. Except for the gold organ pipes and trimming around the stage and on the balcony gratings there is a minimum of decoration, unless you happen to glance up at the statues surrounding the auditorium high above the second balcony. Although the niches were important aspects of the entire acoustical scheme, the addition of the undraped statues was a happy afterthought; and to those of prudish instincts let me add that they were selected by a committee of two hundred proper Bostonians headed by the most proper Mrs. J. W. Elliot. When Symphony Hall was opened for its first concert, in September 1900, these statues were not yet in place, but were added gradually as they came from the studio of Pietro Caproni of Boston.

They represent figures of ancient Rome and Greece and add much to the dignity of the hall, notwithstanding the disparaging remarks usually made by farsighted New Yorkers. To us in the orchestra they have become old friends who give no greeting and expect none. We know they are there guarding our cultural heritage, and we hardly ever look up at them. I dare say there are some of my colleagues who have never even noticed them. After 43 years in the orchestra, Benny Fiedler did notice them once during a Pops concert. "Look, Bixen," he exclaimed during the final measures of Handel's "Largo," as he suddenly looked up at the Amazon of Polycletus, "She's scratching herself!" Then, as we came to the final G-major chord, he exclaimed, "And the other one. He has no pants!"

There are five chandeliers on the ceiling of Symphony Hall, one in each corner and a larger one in the center. The corner ones have four tiers of spokes; the middle one has five. Each of the spokes contains an electric light bulb on its end. During moments of less than full concentration at concerts (especially in choral works when the orchestra has nothing to play), I have wickedly attempted to count the light bulbs–and never quite made it. Our electrician at Symphony Hall has supplied me with the following facts: Each of the corner chandeliers contains 71 spokes and bulbs, while the center one has 111, making a total of 395. The bulbs are changed twice a year–before the symphony season begins in the fall and before the Pops season in the spring. For a long time I wondered, as have other detached music lovers, how in the world this was done. Did someone have to climb up on a ladder? It would be a dizzying height. And where would one get such a ladder? My curiosity was appeased when I came into the hall one day before the opening of the season in September and saw all the chandeliers resting on the floor, suspended by a cable. And that's how it's done!

Just recently the entire hall was repainted. This is no ordinary undertaking. In order to get to the ceiling a scaffold had to be erected which took the better part of a week and cost $35,000. The paint and colors were the same used in the original construction back in 1900, for with Bostonian foresight the planners of Symphony Hall had preserved the original paint formula and color samples. (Even so, one supersensitive music critic detected a change in the acoustical qualities after the hall was repainted.)

Until recently, the lower maroon walls of the hall were painted green every spring for the Pops season, then repainted maroon for the winter concerts. This used to be accomplished miraculously overnight by our building crew. Since the hall was built in 1900 and each year two coats of paint were added, a little figuring will produce the startling fact that the lower walls of Symphony Hall carry over a hundred and thirty coats of paint. No wonder some of our older subscribers have voiced the opinion that the hall seems to be getting narrower!

ENTRANCE EXAM

How does one become a member of the B.S.O.? It isn't easy. First, there must be a vacancy, which, in an orchestra like the Boston Symphony does not occur too often. And when a vacancy does occur, there are usually at least two dozen applicants. Unlike any other profession or business, references, diplomas, or degrees don't count. You have to audition and conductors are cynical. "Let's hear you play!" is their motto. Of course there are exceptions. Our fine violist, Eugene Lehner, was engaged by Serge Koussevitzky solely on Lehner's reputation as a member of the famous Kolisch String Quartet, a quartet which played together for thirteen years, playing from memory the entire chamber-music literature including contemporary works. Lehner signed his contract without playing a note for Koussevitzky.

Auditions are usually horrible affairs. I vividly remember my own inquisition. Koussevitzky was seated in the center, a group of solemn pallbearers all around him. These were the section leaders of the orchestra, who were there to advise

Koussey, but whose advice he rarely took. After I had played a concerto (Arthur Fiedler was my piano accompanist) I was given the inevitable sight-reading test. First there was an easy slow movement from a Mozart symphony, evidently to test my sense of phrasing and ability to heed the dynamics. Then came a more difficult movement from a Brahms symphony, then a Richard Strauss tone poem, then some Stravinsky. And then Dr. Koussevitzky asked the librarian to bring a symphony by Taneyev, of whom I had never even heard. While I was struggling with it, Koussevitzky kept looking at the other members of the jury with a fiendish glee. "Very good!" he exclaimed. "You have never played dat?" And I knew he was making fun of me. He said, "Thank you!" and I packed up my violin, going home to commit suicide. An hour later, however, the manager called to tell me my contract would be ready in a day or so.

Whenever a vacancy occurs in the B.S.O., our personnel manager advertises the fact in all the trade journals. Then, after applications have been received, a date is set for auditions. While Charles Munch was the director of the orchestra, he instituted a system designed to be as fair as possible to all and this system is still used today. Each applicant plays behind a curtain on the stage of Symphony Hall, unknown and unseen by the jury, made up of players of the orchestra. Each contestant has a number and his or her name is known only to the personnel manager. From whatever number of contestants three or four are invited to play again, this time with the conductor joining the jury. If the jury cannot agree, it is the conductor who decides. This system of unseen contestants probably accounts for the fact that we now have four women members of the orchestra. No one knew they were women except the personnel manager, who had wisely and fairly asked them to remove their high-heeled shoes before walking onto the stage!

Years ago, before the present system was established, we needed a new first clarinetist and auditions were held not only in Boston, but also in New York. Munch and a jury of first players were seated in Carnegie Hall to listen to a number of clarinetists. Each came on stage in a state of nervousness, some more nervous than others, went through his ordeal, and left. One of the applicants was Gino Cioffi, an excellent clarinetist who had played under many famous conductors and who was certain that the Boston Symphony needed him more than he needed it. Cioffi came to the center of the stage, clarinet in hand, and said, "Good morning, gentlemen, what do ya wanna hear?"

Munch asked, "What have you prepared?"

"Anything you want—concerto, symphony, opera—anything!"

Munch asked, "Do you play the Mozart Concerto?"

"*Ma* sure!" answered Cioffi. And at this point he beckoned to his pianist and they gave a brilliant performance of the first movement. Finishing with a flourish, Cioffi walked to the edge of the stage and said, "Pretty good, uh?"

Munch turned to Richard Burgin, our concertmaster, and said, "Such confidence! We must have this man!" and Cioffi is still with us.

Sometimes chance plays a role in the manner in which a musician enters the orchestra. For instance, one of our percussion players came into the orchestra without meaning to. Some years ago when our tympanist retired, a number of applicants from all over the country came to play for the job. One of these, a tympanist from New York, played as one of his audition pieces a composition for solo tympani accompanied by various other percussion instruments, having brought with him, at his own expense, a young man to play these instruments. The tympanist did not get the job, but the young man so impressed Mr. Munch and the jury that he was engaged on the spot. There is now an unwritten law among all percussion players: "When you audition for a job, go alone!"

The system of orchestra auditions is, in the opinion of many, not a perfect one; many factors, impossible to ascertain at an audition, go into the making of a good orchestral player—his ensemble ability, his sense of rhythm when playing with the whole orchestra, his ability to follow the conductor, his rapport with fellow players, and his sense of dynamics. (It takes a long time for an inexperienced player to learn to play without hearing himself.) For these reasons a new player in the Boston

Symphony is accepted on a one-year probationary basis, during which time the conductor can judge all of his qualities not immediately apparent at an audition. Not even all good soloists are good orchestra musicians. Once the great Fritz Kreisler sat in on a Boston Symphony rehearsal at the last desk of second violins and later admitted, "I was lost immediately!"

THE DISTAFF SIDE OF THE B.S.O.

Until 1951 there were no females in the Boston Symphony Orchestra. Even our two harpists, the traditional exceptions, were men. The barrier was broken in that year, however, when Olivia Luetcke was engaged as second harpist, and in the following year, upon the retirement of the celebrated Georges Laurent, a second woman was engaged as first flutist. Doriot Anthony Dwyer became the first and, so far, only woman ever to hold such a position. She comes by it naturally as the grandniece of Susan B. Anthony, another lady who broke tradition.

We now have four ladies in the orchestra, flute, piccolo, cello, and harp, and no doubt will have more in the future, whether we men like it or not. Whatever objections we have are purely emotional, for the women in the B.S.O. are excellent players and won their positions simply because they outplayed all the other applicants. The proportion of women in symphony orchestras is constantly growing, and in some of the smaller orchestras it is about fifty per cent.

No particular problems have arisen because of the ladies. When we travel, they are given a dressing room apart from the men where three of them change into their formal playing clothes. The harpist usually changes in her harp trunk which contains her clothes and various convenient appurtenances—except running water. The acceptance of women into symphony orchestras has meant the demise of the all-woman orchestra, an anachronism in today's integration of the sexes. The women's symphony orchestras of the past, some of them quite good, were formed out of necessity and no longer have an artistic usefulness.

As for women conductors, so far the tiny number of aspirants have received little encouragement from orchestra boards, musicians, or the public. There have been some in the past who have enjoyed a modicum of success, notably the late Ethel Leginska, an Englishwoman who changed her name from Leggins, smoked cigars, and conducted with masculine vigor.

The Boston Symphony has been conducted only once by a woman, the celebrated and sagacious French teacher of many composers, Nadia Boulanger, who was invited to conduct a program honoring the memory of her compatriot, Gabriel Fauré. It was a concert of cherished memory.

Among the wives of the Boston Symphony players there is a caste system stronger than among the men themselves. In the orchestra the old monarchial system of first-, second-, and third-class citizens has slowly given way to a more democratic form. Nowadays it is not unusual for a first player to be seen occasionally conversing with a "tutti" player, but "solo" wives do not usually consort with "tutti" wives.

Most of the orchestra news comes from the wives. They seem to have all the secret information about what is going to happen long before it happens. If I want to know about future soloists, conductors, programs, I ask my wife, and if she doesn't know, she calls another wife, who calls another wife, and soon the "official" information is obtained.

Musicians' wives are very protective and zealous of their husbands' abilities and prestige in the orchestra. I overheard one wife say to a friend, "My husband plays just as good as Heifetz, only he never had Heifetz's maazel [luck]."

JUST LITTLE THINGS

At a special rehearsal called by Koussevitzky one evening to rehearse new works, we were close to bedlam. He had not had much chance, if any, to look over the scores and the orchestra had certainly never seen the music before. During the rehearsal, after we had finished a piece in which most of us were lost including the conductor, our second oboist, Jean Devergie, asked the first oboist, Fernand Gillet, what was next, and when Gillet pointed to his part to show him, Devergie said, "My God! I just played it!"

Does anything ever go wrong during a concert? Just little things. Once when we were playing Strauss' Domestic Symphony with Fritz Reiner as conductor, the tympanist discovered the middle page of his part was missing. He did not discover it until we were well into the second page. At about the same time Rolland Tapley, the inside man on the second desk of first violins, turned the page to discover the tympani part in his music. He glanced over at the tympanist, Roman Sculcz, who had turned green and, having a few bars rest, was frantically thumbing through the rest of the music on his stand. Tapley, undaunted, picked up the part and, coattails flying, made a dash toward Sculcz, on his way brushing aside four viola players, a pair of oboists, a contrabassoonist, and three trumpeters, but arriving at the grateful Sculcz's kettles in the nick of time. Meanwhile Reiner and the rest of us thought Tapley had gone berserk and, as Reiner later acknowledged, he thought of stopping the orchestra and running for his life! I must say, in fairness to the librarians, that the misplaced sheet of music was Sculcz's own fault. Before the concert he had taken his music over to the first violins to check a cue and had inadvertently left his part.

A less dramatic but more embarrassing incident took place one evening during a concert at Sanders Theatre in Cambridge when, during a vigorous tremolo passage in the violas, Lehner's bow flew out of his hand into the lap of a lady in the first row. At the time Koussevitzky's eyes were fixed upon the violas and Lehner, without batting an eye, kept on with his tremolo, moving his imaginary bow fast and furiously! Koussey did not even notice what had happened and a few bars later when he turned to the other side of the stage, the lady returned the bow to a very embarrassed Lehner.

During one of the Metropolitan Opera's annual visits to Boston a number of years ago a group of us from the B.S.O. strings were engaged as extra players for the palace scene in Mozart's "Don Giovanni." Since we were to appear on the stage, playing the famous minuet, we were asked to come early to the Opera House for rehearsal and costuming. We arrived at the stage door and were told to go upstairs to the third floor to be fitted—powdered wigs, tunics, and silk britches. The Italian property man was in a foul mood. All of the costumes were too small, and he seemed to put the blame on us. "Why they have to send me giants?" he kept muttering.

As each man was suited, complaining that he could hardly play in such tight-fitting clothes, the property man kept getting more and more exasperated. By the time my turn came I was determined to say nothing, whether or not my costume fit. He slipped a coat on my back, and with great difficulty buttoned up the front while I held my breath; but the collar would not come together no matter how we both tried. "Am I gonna have trouble with you, too?" he mumbled. He ripped off the coat and said, "Let's try it backwards." I held my arms out, put them through the sleeves, and he went to work furiously buttoning it up the back while I held my breath again and perspired profusely. He was able to fasten the collar in back while my eyes almost popped out of my head. I made a gesture with my arms indicating that it was impossible to play in this damned coat. He looked at me and said, "'At's awright. You no gotta play a concerto. Joost a few notes." And he sang the minuet in a croaking falsetto voice. "It's a good enough!" Then we tried on the trousers, which wouldn't even come together at the waist. When I looked at him beseechingly, he said, "'At's good enough. When you play on the stage, you on a balcony and the balcony has a fence in front of you, about so high. So don't sit up straight. Slouch down a little and you be awright."

We then went to another room where an assistant coach put us through a very perfunctory rehearsal, and instructed us to keep our eyes on the conductor, Bruno Walter, all the while we were on stage. Nothing was said about our doing anything on stage except playing.

Before the palace scene opened we were all seated on the stage balcony. When the curtain rose, I was momentarily blinded by the footlights and frantically searched for Mr. Walter, whom I found about a mile away in the pit. Next to me was a cellist, a member of the Met orchestra, an old-timer who had "played" this role many times, and who was supposed to have instructed me on what to do, which he hadn't.

During our playing of the minuet there was a sudden scream as Zerlina repulsed the advances of the lecherous Don Giovanni. It scared me out of my wits. The cellist next to me got up from his chair, leaned over the balcony, and said, "Oh my God!"

"What happened?" I asked frantically, as Don Giovanni dragged Leporello onto the stage, and all the guests looked upon them with horror, including my cellist colleague.

"Nutting," he answered, still looking horrified, and out of the corner of his mouth he said, "I'm acting!" This broke me up, and I couldn't help laughing. At this point Herbert Graf, the eminent stage director of the Met, saw me from the wings and shouted, "It is not to laugh!" then ordered us all to leave the stage. I don't know, to this day, whether or not we were supposed to stay all through the act. One thing I do know; we were never again asked to appear in "Don Giovanni."

Bostonians will always remember the late Bernard Fiedler, Arthur's uncle and an institution in himself. A bachelor, he had been in the orchestra longer than anyone else, and over the years had become a bit cynical. He had an acid wit and his favorite pastime was walking around the tuning room listening to his colleagues' practicing. Invariably he would shake his head disdainfully and say, "The technique is pretty good, but produce me a tone!"

During my second week in the orchestra we played Tchaikovsky's Sixth Symphony, the "Pathétique," on Friday afternoon in Symphony Hall. At the very end of the piece, when the violins have stopped playing and the lower strings take over to bring the symphony to its quiet, sad ending, we had been admonished by Koussevitzky to sit with heads bowed until the piece was over. This Sixth Symphony was a great favorite of Koussevitzky's, one which, I am sure, he subconsciously felt he himself had composed, and at the end he always had tears in his eyes. I looked up, saw the tears, and felt the emotion in the hall, the electric stillness of the audience and, being new in the orchestra, was tremendously affected by it all. Suddenly Benny said, "Dickson, you like my new shoes?"

The late Joseph Leibovici sat directly behind me in the first violin section. Over the years he had taken to muttering to himself during concerts and rehearsals, and some of his remarks have become classics. After we had sawed through the long Schubert C Major Symphony on an unbearably hot day, he said, "Damn Schubert! He wrote two symphonies, one unfinished and the other endless!" Leibovici's discontent showed itself in other ways. Once while we were rehearsing the "Spring Symphony" of Schumann, Koussevitzky turned to the violins and said, "Gentlemen, be happy. Be gay!" Joseph immediately answered, under his breath, "What's the occasion?" And after the funeral of one of our colleagues Munch praised the string quartet that had played at the services. "The Beethoven was beautiful," he said, "but a little too slow." Leibovici retorted, "At the next funeral they will play it faster."

Jean LeFranc, our former first violist, was a quiet, unassuming Frenchman who, although he had lived in this country for a number of years, knew nothing about the United States. For him the Boston Symphony was the United States and what went on outside did not concern him. One Sunday afternoon in Pittsburgh we had Frank Sinatra in the audience and during intermission he came backstage to be greeted by a number of the musicians. "Mais oui, I know the Franck Sonata," he said, "but who is this man?"

For many years one of the landmarks of the symphony was the venerable Einar Hansen, Danish violinist, who sat four rows back of the concertmaster in the first violins on the outside. He was a small, extremely energetic man who always fiddled furiously, and his white, flowing hair stood out above the whole orchestra. He was the cynosure of all eyes and, indeed, after the Friday-afternoon ladies took their seats at the beginning of the concert, they would unconsciously look for Hansen. He rarely missed a concert, but whenever he was not in his usual place, the Symphony Hall switchboard would be flooded with inquiries. His distinguished appearance often caused strangers in out-of-town railroad stations and airports to think he was the conductor. In a Pullman dining car a lady sitting at Koussevitzky's table, aware that the Boston Symphony was aboard, pointed at Hansen at the next table and asked Koussevitzky, "Is that the conductor?" much to Koussey's chagrin. Hansen was, and still is, an amazing phenomenon of energy. He played in the orchestra until he was in his late seventies (some say he was even eighty) without ever showing any sign of diminishing activity. He was an L Street Brownie, one of a group of hardy winter swimmers, and he took a dip in the ocean every morning before the rehearsal, even in sub-zero weather. Hansen never seemed to rest and even during intermissions he could be seen furiously fiddling away in a corner of the tuning room.

He was blissfully unaware of the outside world and lived in a kind of ivory tower. One night when I was conducting the Pops, one of our Trustees, Michael T. Kelliher, brought Jack Benny and we prevailed upon him to perform with us. He borrowed a violin from one of the orchestra men, the librarian hurriedly supplied the orchestra parts, and Benny came out to play the "Czardas" of Monti. After he had played a few bars, Hansen turned to his partner and exclaimed, "He is not a good player! Why did they ask him to play?"

The backstage atmosphere of the Boston Symphony has changed considerably during the past thirty years. No longer is there the profusion of foreign languages. Today everyone speaks English. The history of the orchestra can be divided into three periods, the German period from its beginning in 1881 when the orchestra was predominantly German, including conductors; then the French period, beginning in 1918 and remaining so until the middle of the Koussevitzky era; then gradually a more and more American period, until now even baseball is discussed, the performance of the Red Sox having a profound effect upon the performance of the B.S.O. One evening at a party following a concert in Tanglewood Charles Munch asked if someone would explain the game of baseball to him. There were three volunteers, Isaac Stern, Leonard Bernstein, and Eugene Istomin, and for the next half hour they expounded the art of Abner Doubleday in the language of Voltaire and Victor Hugo. I heard someone say, "Le pitcher jete le bal et vous le frappez et run like hell à first base." It was getting more and more complicated and incomprehensible to Munch, and finally they gave up when no one could explain a squeeze-play in French.

Years ago our fine French cellist Paul Tortelier came to the United States with his mother and neither one spoke more than three words of English. After they had been here about a year Tortelier told me that he and his mother had attended night school the past season. At the end of the semester there was a kind of mock graduation. The principal called the Torteliers into his office and explained that since Paul had missed so many classes, he could not be graduated, but his mother who had attended every class would be graduated with honors. She did not understand a word and Tortelier had to translate.

One of the most lovable members of the B.S.O. was our former first violist, Joseph dePasquale. As well as being a fine chef, Joe is one of the great violists of our time, with a healthy and robust sound and solid technique and an instinctive musical sense. These two great talents make his life quite complete, but apart from these he has few interests, none of them cultural. Although born and raised in this country, he has never cultivated the habit of grammatical speech and in the B.S.O. he was known as "Mister Malaprop." Once after he had heard me talk at one of our pre-symphony affairs, he said to me, "I didn't know you were so literal."

Just before the birth of his first child I was sitting with him in a restaurant in New York. "When do you expect the baby, Joe?" I asked.

"Any day now," he said.

"Joe," I said, "don't do what I did. When our first baby was born, we waited so long to go to the hospital that the baby was almost born on the way."

"Oh," he said, "what's so terrible? If the baby comes, all you got to do is cut the biblical cord!"

Hugh Ross, the celebrated conductor of the Schola Cantorum in New York, was conducting a choral concert with us one day. Ross is a very volatile conductor who constantly moves his hands rapidly while conducting. After a few minutes Joe turned to his partner and said, "This guy conducts like he had celebrated palsy!"

The day of the absent-minded, introverted musician is, in keeping with the general trend of the world, almost gone by. The young musician of today is worldly, articulate, alert, and perhaps a little less idealistic. He would have to go far to match the dedication of a Louis Speyer, our former English-horn player of the orchestra, who retired a few years ago after forty-seven years of service without ever missing a concert or rehearsal. Somehow the absent-minded musician of the past always managed to remember his primary commitment to his job.

One absent-minded member of the orchestra now is our first violist, Burton Fine, a brilliant young man and wonderful player, who is so preoccupied that he hardly ever greets anyone. He recently came to me before a rehearsal and asked if I had seen him come in. When I answered in the affirmative, he asked, "Was I carrying my viola case?"

"Yes, I think so," I said.

"Well, then," he said, "it must be here somewhere."

CONCERTMASTER

Richard Burgin has a keen, analytical mind, a warm, vibrant personality, and a wealth of knowledge, musical and otherwise. For over forty years he was the revered concertmaster of the Boston Symphony and also a great bridge player (at one time ranking player of Massachusetts), an inveterate gambler, and a student of politics. Koussevitzky had enormous respect for him and used to say of him, "He has an abstractical mind."

Richard was also absent-minded. On the day of a concert in Worcester, about forty miles from Boston, he taught all afternoon. Suddenly he realized how late it was so he dressed hurriedly and drove to the Back Bay railroad station. Finding no place to park near the station, he drove some distance, parked the car, and hailed a taxi. At the station he gave the driver a bill and hurried for the train. Once aboard he found his accompanist and they sat down together. When the conductor approached them for the tickets, Richard reached into his pocket to discover that he had given the taxi driver a twenty-dollar bill

Richard Burgin, former Concertmaster of the Boston Symphony.
Photograph by Milton Feinberg.

and had no more money. The accompanist paid the fare. In Worcester they discovered that they did not know where the concert was to be given, but Richard remembered a student of his who lived in Worcester. A call was made to her and fortunately she knew. When they arrived at the hall, Richard opened his violin case to discover he had no bow. So another call was made to the pupil and she obliged by bringing hers.

At a party for Richard, given to him by his colleagues in honor of his twenty-fifth anniversary as concertmaster of the B.S.O., much was said about the fact that for twenty-five years he had been borrowing mutes and losing them. A large mute was hung around his neck with a chain, then a bagful of mutes was presented to him. The next morning at rehearsal he turned to Julius Theodorowicz, his partner, and asked, "Do you have an extra mute?"

What is a concertmaster? The term goes back to the eighteenth century when the role of a conductor was a secondary one. He was merely brought in by the musicians to beat time, but the over-all musical responsibility was in the hands of the first violinist, the "master of the concert." While the role of the conductor has become paramount in an orchestra, the term "concertmaster" has remained to designate the first of the first violinists, the player in the orchestra second in command to the conductor. He is the man who sits immediately to the left of the conductor and who "leads" the first-violin section. Indeed, in England he is called the "leader."

The duties of a concertmaster are varied and are slightly different in every orchestra, depending upon the personality of the conductor. Some conductors rely heavily upon the musical advice of their concertmaster, delegating to him a great deal of authority, while others brook no interference in their own singular authority.

First of all, the concertmaster must be the best violinist in the orchestra, of virtuoso caliber since he is frequently called upon to appear as soloist. If a composition is scored for passages or cadenzas by a single violin, it is the concertmaster who plays them.

It is also the concertmaster's job to arrange the bowings of the string section according to the conductor's musical interpretation. (When you go to a symphony concert and are fascinated by the drill-like perfection of all the string players moving their bowing arms up and down simultaneously, it is the concertmaster who has prescribed the directions ahead of time.)

The concertmaster may be called upon to rehearse certain sections of the orchestra, particularly the strings, when there are technically difficult problems and in some orchestras he is eventually designated as the associate or assistant conductor. The concertmaster's role in an orchestra is a psychologically difficult one. He is both a player and a leader and, as such, must tread the tightrope of diplomacy in dealing with his colleagues on one hand and the conductor on the other.

Our present concertmaster, Joseph Silverstein, is a remarkable man. Though comparatively young, still in his thirties, he possesses a musical maturity far beyond his years. Innately gifted, he has an astounding "phonographic" memory and is able to reproduce whatever music he hears. He once played the difficult "Carmen Fantasy" of Waxman with the Pops after having learned it entirely from a Heifetz recording without even seeing the score. I once played a Schubert quartet with him when he played the entire piece without turning a page. In the orchestra his knowledge of the score is uncanny, and even in piano concertos he can instantly reproduce the soloists' parts at any given point. I once heard him accompany on the violin one of his students in a Mozart concerto in which he played all of the leading orchestral voices.

According to custom, Silverstein began his career with the Boston Symphony on the last stand of second violins while still in his early twenties, then broke all precedent by moving steadily up to the concertmaster's chair. Nowhere else, in any other orchestra, has this ever happened, yet nowhere else has it been more deserved.

Add to Silverstein's talent an almost superhuman capacity for hard work, and you have one of the great concertmasters of our day. Joe Silverstein, a bright and articulate person, has, like most of our young American-trained musicians, a variety of outside interests. He is well-informed, plays an excellent game of bridge, golf or squash, and is a rabid baseball fan. He also has a healthy set of nerves. Recently, just before he was due to play the Bruch "Scottish Fantasy" at a Friday-afternoon performance, Leinsdorf came into the greenroom to summon him and found him fast asleep on the couch.

The inevitable comparisons are made between Silverstein and his predecessor, Richard Burgin, and these are difficult to define. An orchestra's concertmaster is molded in the image of the conductor, his personality, his methods, and his desires. Koussevitzky allowed and tolerated no comments or suggestions from anyone during rehearsals, even from the concertmaster. On the other hand Erich Leinsdorf expects and welcomes Silverstein's suggestions, even corrections; and this has caused some resentment on the part of the players. An orchestra player has the need to look up to one central authority, one all-knowing father-figure. Division of authority seems to carry seeds of rebellion and lowering of morale, regardless of the esteem, or lack of it, held by the players for either the concertmaster or conductor. Undoubtedly the Boston Symphony's new conductor, William Steinberg, will have his own views on the role of the concertmaster.

CONDUCTOR

Wearing two hats as I do as player and occasional conductor presents some problems. No matter how affable, how comradely, how unpretentious I try to be with my colleagues, I am looked upon with suspicion. I am on the "other side." I am a potential enemy. As a member of the orchestra I find myself in the awkward position of being my own enemy—and hating myself for it. I am also becoming quite

Joseph Silverstein, present Concertmaster. Photograph by Milton Feinberg.

paranoid and whenever I conduct the orchestra, I tend to become more so. My dearest colleagues seem to become metamorphosed snarling beasts if I as much glance at them, even if my glance is a complimentary one. One night while I was conducting the Pops in a piano concerto, Pat Cardillo, our illustrious first clarinetist, missed an entrance. I tried to convey by a friendly glance that it could happen to anyone, but afterwards he not only blamed me for his mistake, but insisted I tried to belittle him. No amount of denial on my part would placate him.

Whenever I am scheduled to conduct, at least a half-dozen members will jokingly ask me for the night off. On the night of the Marciano-Walcott fight, I excused more than half the orchestra! One of my colleagues has hated me for years because *I* dared to be upset when, an hour before a concert, he telephoned to say he had just heard of the death of an aunt in Paris two days earlier, and *he* was too upset to play. Another colleague, a violinist, refuses to use vibrato unless I pay him fifty cents for each concert. Matt Ruggiero, bassoonist, after we had been stoned at a Franklin Park concert, came to me and said, "No wonder they threw stones. You didn't make the repeat in the first movement of the symphony!"

The role of a conductor in an orchestra has been so firmly established that it always surprises me when I am asked, "What does the conductor do? What do you musicians need him for? You are all professionals. You have the music in front of you. Why can't you play without him?" The answers apparently aren't as obvious as they seem.

Over the past one hundred and fifty years the position of conductor has risen in stature from that of mere time beater to complete overlord. The one man of every orchestra who never produces a sound or a note of music has become the all-important ingredient, and the highest paid. He is the one who attempts to impose his will upon one hundred men and it is his personality that distinguishes one orchestra from another.

From a practical standpoint the conductor is more important to the players today than he was in the eighteenth-century or-

A rare meeting of three successive Boston Symphony conductors–Pierre Monteux, Serge Koussevitzky, and Charles Munch. Photograph by John Brook.

chestra. If these small ensembles found it difficult to play together without a time beater, how much more difficult it would be for our present-day enormous orchestras. If only for the purpose of playing together the conductor is necessary. While it is true that a professional orchestra could stay together quite well in baroque and classical music, and even in some of the romantic music, it would be catastrophic to attempt any rhythmically complicated music of the twentieth century without a conductor. There have been so-called conductorless orchestras in the past.

One appeared in Moscow a number of years ago but it was short-lived. Another functioned in New York for a brief period.

Actually there can be no music of any kind without direction. Whether the director sits or stands, whether he plays or waves a baton, the primary impulse must come from somebody. Chamber music is played without a conductor, yet even in a string quartet someone must lead. Four men could not possibly start together by mental telepathy. True, at times each one may take over the role as leader, but direction there must be. Even when only two play together one must lead, the other acquiesce, and the role of conductor can change constantly from one to the other. (Occasionally even a conductor learns to follow. Pierre Monteux used to say, "It is the wise conductor who knows when to follow the orchestra.")

The mere physical distance of one player from another in a modern symphony orchestra makes it difficult, and sometimes impossible, for players to hear each other, and for this reason alone the conductor is necessary, as a means of producing for the eye what cannot be achieved by the ear. I am told that French horn players sometimes cannot hear anyone except themselves. (Notice how unfortunately impractical are their unwieldy sidesaddle instruments that blow into each other's ears.)

An orchestra without a conductor, no matter how many rehearsals it could afford, no matter how well it could learn to play together, would become at best a musical machine without a heart or soul. There would be no spontaneity, no spark of human inspiration. True, the composer indicates all the tempo marks either by words (allegro, andante, lento, etc.) or by metronomic numbers. But who is to determine at the exact moment of performance how fast is allegro, or how slow is lento, or exactly the speed of a metronomic indication? Then there are the considerations of expression and nuance. How loud is forte, or how soft is pianissimo? Add to these the all-important problems of balance, and the conductor's role becomes indispensable. Who in our large modern orchestras except the man on the podium can determine the exact balance between the different choirs of the orchestra? Who, but one, standing before his

Erich Leinsdorf conducting the Boston Symphony. Photograph by Milton Feinberg.

human instrument, can be given the responsibility of judging whether or not the brasses are overpowering the woodwinds, or whether the accompaniment is too loud for the leading voice? These are considerations entirely in the hands of the conductor. Add to these those intangible qualities of inspiration which some conductors have, of achieving the full potential of the music and the composer's intentions, and of bringing out the full capabilities of their players, and, indeed, to make them surpass themselves. Then you have the almost but not quite complete duties of a conductor.

There is also the matter of a conductor's sense of hearing. We musicians are sometimes asked, "Does the conductor really know when you play a wrong note?" Some do and some don't. There is a tuning-room story about a mediocre conductor who came to a fine professional orchestra and, in order to impress them with his hearing, purposely put wrong notes into the parts so that he could stop and correct them. At the rehearsal, however, everything seemed to be right. Finally, after a loud chord in the brasses he stopped the orchestra and said, "The fourth horn played an F-sharp. Please change it to F-natural." The horn player replied, "Maestro, some damn fool put in an F-sharp, but I know the music. I *did* play an F-natural!"

The late Italian conductor Victor deSabata once came to Tanglewood to conduct a concert, and he impressed all of us with his uncanny ability to pick out wrong notes in "thick" chords. He even corrected a note in a work we had been playing wrongly for years. DeSabata was a fine conductor, immensely conceited, and capable of becoming quite nasty. At one point in the rehearsal he accused a clarinetist of playing a false note. The clarinetist tried to argue with him (a musician's privilege only with guest conductors), but deSabata cut him short. "Please, my dear man," he said, "the finest doctors in Europe have proclaimed my ears to be perfect!" And the matter was settled. Orchestra players constantly complain about conductors, and baseball players complain about managers, but they remain a necessary evil.

Orchestra players are frequently asked to give their opinions about conductors; yet what they think doesn't really matter. A very fine Western orchestra engaged a conductor a number of years ago entirely on the enthusiastic recommendation of the players, and he almost ruined the orchestra. This conductor was loved by the musicians, he bent over backward to please them, and they tried to please him; but his limited abilities soon estranged him from both audience and critics, and he left after a comparatively short tenure.

The situation is quite different in European orchestras, where orchestra musicians have traditionally had a hand in choosing

The newly appointed Music Director of the Boston Symphony, William Steinberg, at a rehearsal. Photograph by Ed Fitzgerald.

their conductors, and it seems to work over there. Some day it will work in this country also, for it is fast becoming apparent that the old system of orchestral dictatorships with tyrannical, quasi-maniacal conductors can no longer be tolerated. Certainly musicians can make mistakes in their choice of conductors, but so can nonmusical trustees.

Throughout its long existence the trustees of the Boston Symphony Orchestra have never consulted any of its players in the choosing of a conductor, and they have been extraordinarily lucky. For the most part they have chosen wisely and well; yet there comes a time when changes in thinking inevitably take place, when the judgment of the musicians must be considered, when an orchestra board can work together with a responsible representation of the players in choosing a leader to the mutual benefit of all. The present board of trustees of the Boston Symphony Orchestra has changed its thinking quite radically over the past years and is now actually beginning to consult the players not only in their choice of conductor, but in matters of general musical policy. This will, of course, put great responsibility upon the shoulders of the players, and only the future will tell whether or not our American musicians can live up to the maturity and self-discipline of their European colleagues.

What do musicians look for in a conductor? First of all, he must know the musical score; and he must know it better than any of the players. An orchestra soon loses respect for a conductor whom it must teach. Secondly, the conductor must have the power to communicate his wishes and to inspire his players to give beyond themselves. (Serge Koussevitzky had this power to an enormous degree.) Musicians respond, sometimes in spite of themselves, through respect or through fear, although the latter consideration has become less of a factor since the advent of stronger musicians' unions and the scarcity of good players. A conductor must not talk too much. The late Pierre Monteux used to constantly admonish his conducting pupils, "Talk less and conduct more! They will not listen anyway." Time and again we have been exposed to the garrulousness of a conductor who, in his efforts to show how much he knows, talks so much that the music itself is forgotten. This conductor stops, like an alcoholic, at every bar, to explain the value of an eighth note, or the duration of a quarter; and at the end of a movement he will recapitulate by talking, pointing out what was out of tune, which instruments were too loud, which too soft, etc., etc., while the bored musicians look at their watches.

The eminent Viennese maestro, Josef Krips, who conducted the Boston Symphony for the first time at Tanglewood in the summer of 1968, made a very deep impression upon the orchestra. He not only "knew" his scores thoroughly, but he knew how to rehearse. His first words to the orchestra were, "I will not make speeches, but I hope we will communicate through the music." He is a large, roly-poly man, bald, with a jolly and expressive face; and he seems to love music with a passion that is infectious. His method of rehearsing is to correct things immediately, then to go on without long discourses, and upon occasion even to shout out his admonitions—during the music—"Listen to the oboe!" "Brass! Don't cover the strings!"

Perhaps the worst morale-destroying habit of a conductor is that of delegating authority to leaders of sections. Playing in an orchestra is subjugation enough of a musician's personality, but having to take orders from more than one authority leads to rebellion. Koussevitzky had, through uncanny instinct, the quality of instilling into each player a sense of individuality and self-respect. If something was not to his liking it was corrected on the spot. If a chord in the brass or woodwinds was not in tune it was immediately rehearsed, over and over if necessary, until it was right. If certain passages in the strings were not clean they would be rehearsed, en masse, until they came out right. Leinsdorf's method, on the other hand, is quite different. If something is wrong he will invariably speak only to the leader of the particular section. "Mr. So-and-So, please see to it that this chord is in tune." "Mr. So-and-So, please clean up this passage in your section." For some reason he finds it difficult to address a man directly, and this has led to a feeling of resentment, of class discrimination and "second-class citizenship" among the players, a feeling which in no way lessens their admiration for his musical knowledge.

The history of the Boston Symphony Orchestra will forever be classified into two eras: B.K. (before Koussevitzky) and A.K. (after Koussevitzky). From the time he first came to the orchestra in 1924 through the twenty-five years of his conductorship he was able to establish and maintain an aura of Olympian aloofness and royal untouchability. His sartorial splendor, his beautiful carriage, his reserved but dramatic gestures on the podium, all of these endeared him immediately to the Back Bay ladies. Serge Koussevitzky was an actor, a sincere and wonderful actor who not only portrayed a role but actually lived it and passionately believed in that role. And because the role demanded it, he was able, through his strong will and personality, to achieve, at enormous expense to the orchestra, a level of salary and living far beyond that of any other conductor, before or since. In those early days before the era of plane travel when the orchestra made all its out-of-town trips by train, it was customary on our annual two-week "Western Tour" for the members of the orchestra to ride in Pullman berths while Dr. Koussevitzky and his entourage, consisting of Mrs. K., the valet, the cook, a secretary, and the maid, had an entire car to themselves.

The question of Koussevitzky's musicianship has long been debated by critics, musicologists, and players and I leave the final judgment to posterity. I am convinced he was the greatest conductor who ever lived. Whether or not he was a deeply intellectual student of music, the fact is that he made music, that he felt it through every fiber of his being. It might be said that Koussevitzky approached music first with his heart, then with his mind. He had unfailing musical instincts and instinctive good taste in everything he did. Even when he was wrong he could, through his iron will and dynamic force, convince you that he was right. I have seen him argue with composers over

Serge Koussevitzky by Olga Koussevitzky

their own music and, with rare exceptions, prevail. It was proven time and time again that Koussevitzky could present a composer's work infinitely better than the composer himself.

To him music could not exist without great beauty of sound and he is the only conductor I have ever known who spent hours of rehearsal time practicing sound. We would play certain passages over and over again "until," as he would say, "we will have 'our' sonority." One of his constant pleadings was for "more dolce." Indeed "dolce" became for him a word signifying perfection in music. If there was bad ensemble, he would shout, "Gentlemen, it is awfully not togedder! You must play more dolce." If he thought it was too loud, he would admonish the players to play more softly and "more dolce." If it was too soft, he would say, "I cannot hear the dolce." Not sustained enough? "Gentlemen, please don't made it a low in the music" ("low" was a direct aural translation from German "loch"), "because when you made it a low the dolce was lost!"

Serge Koussevitzky was a man of sincere dedication, enormous ego, and no sense of humor. The latter I discovered, to my dismay, during my first year in the orchestra. The orchestra gave a "fun" party for the benefit of our pension fund. The ballroom of the Somerset Hotel was engaged and the men of the orchestra went to work organizing acts, stunts, performances, and skits. Our dignified concertmaster, Richard Burgin, actually recruited and conducted a jazz group; our first trumpeter, Georges Mager, sang a duet, in costume, with his wife; Emil Kornsand, violinist, did tricks of magic; Einar Hansen, violinist, danced a Russian trepak; there were numerous skits spoofing various musicians, etc., etc. Jacobus Langendoen and I did a barbershop scene. Langendoen was the barber, I the customer, both of us heavily disguised with wigs, false noses, and beards.

I walked into the barbershop with a violin case under my arm and, in what I thought was a disguising accent, said, "Gooda morning, Mister Langendoni, I need a quicka shave. Gotta rehearsal ten o'clock." And as I sat down in the chair and Langendoen began to lather my face we talked.

"Where do you play now?"

"Bostona Symphony."

"Oh, I used to play there, but the conductor called me a shuster, so I decided to become a barber. And I'ma much happier. By the way, who'sa the conductor now?"

And I quickly answered, "I don't know."

"Whatta you mean, you don't know? You just say you play in the orchester, no?"

"Yes, but I minda my own business, I never look the conductor. Somebody's a waving a little stick upa there, but I don't know who he is."

Well, the next morning at rehearsal Koussey told us all how much he had enjoyed the show, but he did not mention the barbershop skit. About six months later, toward the end of the season, we were giving a concert at Sanders Theatre at Harvard and had just finished playing Roussel's Second Symphony before the intermission when, before turning around to bow to the audience, Koussey stared at me for a fleeting moment and shook his head disapprovingly; and as he walked by me, he leaned over and said, "Even if you don't know who the conductor is, you must watch!"

During the following season at a rather trying rehearsal at which nothing seemed to please Koussey he suddenly looked at me and said, "Di ensemble is awfully not togedder. How can it be togedder ven di gentleman don't know who is di conductor!" And these outbursts became periodic. It got so that I was afraid to take my eyes off him, even at the risk of missing notes. Every time Koussey looked down upon the first violins he met my icy stare. Of course he could not very well ask me not to look at him, but I felt that it was becoming uncomfortable even to him. So, one day while we were rehearsing a Haydn symphony, he suddenly stopped and said, "You know, gentlemen, ven ve are playing a classical piece di I know and you know so vell, it is not necessary to look di conductor all di time!" I took the hint.

But that was not the end of it. During the late thirties when only a small select group of the orchestra gave the Tanglewood concerts in the Berkshires, Koussevitsky did not invite me and when I asked our personnel manager the reason, he frankly told me that Koussey had called me a "bad man."

So, about a month before the Tanglewood season I wrote to him in Paris where he was vacationing, praising him to the skies and explaining to him that it had been a bad joke on my part, how could anyone not know who the great Koussevitzky was? that I was sorry, etc. . . . A week later our personnel manager received the following cable from Paris: "Engage Dickson for Tanglewood."

The era of Koussevitzky was an exciting and turbulent one. Almost every rehearsal was a nightmare, every concert a thrilling experience. Those were the days when it was expected of conductors to be tyrannical and temperamental, and Koussevitzky was no exception. During his reign there were in the B.S.O. one hundred and five players and one hundred and six ulcers. (One man had two.) In the vicinity of Symphony Hall in the Back Bay section of Boston there is, within a half-mile area, the greatest concentration of doctors' offices of any similar area in the world. Most of these doctors got their start during the Koussevitzky era. Each rehearsal had its inevitable "scandahl," when Koussey would stop and say, "Ve vill had it a scandahl after a scandahl until ve vill not have dat vat it need!"

But the concerts with Koussevitzky were wonderful. In spite of everything, he had a way of instilling into each musician a kind of pride and self-esteem that made him play better than his own capabilities. I don't remember a concert under Koussevitzky where, at the end, each player was not as soaking wet and emotionally spent as the conductor.

Koussevitzky had an intensively subjective approach to music, all kinds of music, it didn't matter what school, what style, what period. He simply loved music, and whatever he conducted he appropriated as his own, whether it was Tchaikovsky, Beethoven, or Bartók. Whenever he conducted a new work, whether or not he understood it, he would convince himself, and us, that this was the "greatest since Beethoven," and if the audience did not agree with him, he would walk off the stage muttering, "Idiot publicum!" and perhaps never play the piece again. His way with composers was imperious. "Aaron," he would say to Copland in the balcony while we were rehearsing a new work, "vy do you write mezzo-forte? You know mezzo-forte is di most baddest nuance *qui existe*. It must be pianissimo." And Copland would nod in agreement. With other composers he would have occasional difficulties. Hindemith, for example, would not let Koussey alter even one nuance.

Serge Koussevitzky was a born leader and he found it almost impossible to take orders from anybody, musical or otherwise. He was not a good accompanist for soloists, for unless things went his way they were apt not to go at all. I remember the Prokofiev G Minor Violin Concerto with Heifetz in which we finished a half bar after Heifetz, and there were others.

During the Koussevitzky era there were comparatively few soloists with the B.S.O. The glamour of Serge Koussevitzky was great enough to maintain full houses without soloists. And in all the eleven years I played under K. I do not remember an empty seat either in Symphony Hall or any of the other halls we played throughout the country. And such were the encomiums heaped upon him and the orchestra by critics and public that he would have had to be less than human not to have been influenced by it all. No wonder when a dear old lady said to him after a concert, "Doctor Koussevitzky, to us you are God," he answered "I know my responsibility!" There is also a story that after a concert a friend said, "You know, Serge Alexandrovitch, you are not only the greatest conductor, you are the *only* conductor!"

Koussey, pulling himself up, said, "Come now, there are other fine conductors in the world."

"Who?" asked the friend.

"Well . . ." And he turned to his wife: "Natasha, who?"

Koussevitzky's English was not good, but it was somehow more colorful and certainly more descriptive than good English. He came to this country when he was middle-aged. Having left his native Russia and lived in different parts of Europe for many years, he spoke French and German in addition to Russian, but the task of learning a new language was for him a formidable one. Koussevitzky had no talent for languages. Even his French and German were not good. So he bent each language to his own will, twisting and turning it for his own purposes. Syntax and pronunciation were sacrificed to his own ends. Indeed, he developed a style of language that is still quoted today by all who knew him. How can anyone who was there ever forget his opening words at the inauguration of the new shed at Tanglewood. He took a prepared paper from his pocket and, before reading it, said, "Leddies and gentlemen, you vill plizz excuse it di pepper because ven I no have it di pepper I mistake it di langvadge."

Monday-morning rehearsals in the Koussevitzky days were relatively pleasant affairs. At these rehearsals he would invariably go over the programs of the previous Friday-afternoon and Saturday-night concerts, pointing out what was good here, what was bad there, and since there had been enormous success at both concerts (there always was) he was usually in a benign mood. He would rhetorically ask why the oboe did not play "more soft" here, the strings "more dolce" there, not ever expecting an answer. No one ever spoke during a Koussevitzky rehearsal.

Koussevitzky's philosophy about music was simple and to the point. "It must always be dolce, with good tone, with good intonation, and with alive!" He was constantly preoccupied with sound. Once he stopped the orchestra and said, "Gentlemen! A noise is not a beautiful sound. A sound is a dolce who have a beautiful round tone."

Some scholarly conductors might go into long dissertations about the reasons for their musical requests. Koussey was always simple and to the point. He stopped the violas once in the first movement of Brahms' First Symphony and said, "Kinder! Di main thing is ta-ta-ta. But ven it isn't, vot it is?" And they understood.

"Gentlemen," he once exclaimed, "you play all the time the wrong notes not in time! And please made important, you play like it is something nothing!"

Occasionally his words became so mixed up with emotion that they flowed out haphazardly, as "Gentlemen, you are awfully not togedder. You play di notes in time, but vot is between di times you don't care about. Please made it tremendously your attention! And you are awfully bad in tune today. Or too high, or too low. Ve cannot permit us di luxus to be not in tune!"

He could not tolerate nonchalance in the orchestra and no matter how well a man played, if he didn't look the part, he would incur the wrath of Koussey. And after a while the string players learned to swing and sway. Once he said to Gaston Elcus, a violinist who played beautifully but without histrionics, "Please, Mister Elcus, you must not such a negligible way how you played it!" He would literally fly into a rage if he noticed a string player playing without vibrato. "How can you play with died fingers?"

One morning during a rehearsal of the Wagner Tristan Prelude he stopped the orchestra, turned to the violin section, and exclaimed, "The first violins is cold! This music must be very appassionato—full of patience! I don't know how you stay married!"

His temper at times was ungovernable and unpredictable. One Monday morning when he and the orchestra were in a relaxed mood and things seemed to be going smoothly and happily as we ran through Copland's breezy "El Salón México" in preparation for an orchestra tour, he spied a couple of wind players stamping their feet rather heavily and without warning he picked up the score and flung it through the air. He was a pretty bad shot because it landed in the lap of a second fiddler, who sat there transfixed and didn't dare to touch it. Without a word Koussey, purple with rage, left the stage for an unscheduled intermission while Louis Speyer (one of the stompers) went up to Koussey's room to apologize. By this time his anger had subsided and when it was explained to him that the men meant no disrespect for him, but were merely carried away by the music, he smiled like a benevolent father toward his misbehaved children, came back to the podium—and canceled the rest of the rehearsal.

He was so unpredictable that no one ever knew where he stood with him. A compliment today could turn into a scathing denunciation tomorrow. Words of praise for the playing of a

musical phrase could suddenly turn into harsh criticism. In the "Russian Easter Overture" of Rimsky-Korsakov the second trombone has a declamatory solo. After Lucien Hansotte had played it, Koussey stopped and said, "Mister Hansotte, I have played this overture many times with many orchestras. Never have I heard it played better!" We all scuffled our feet in the traditional manner of applause and Hansotte beamed. But not for long.

"Ah nuh, let us made it again," said Koussey and this time before Hansotte was able to get through the first two notes Koussey said, "It is a little too loud. Let us try again." The next attempt was "too soft." The next "out of tune," and the next "bad sound," and the next "bad conception," until Hansotte fell apart completely. "You know," said Koussey, "it is the worst played I have ever heard!"

Koussevitzky had a high regard for all of his musicians. "You are all great artists!" he would say over and over again and he was so convincing that it was difficult not to believe him. He was concerned about the health of each man, not in a personal, but in a possessive way. These were "his" players, his own stable of racehorses who, if treated well, would perform better. Before a trip he would admonish us not to eat bad food, to dress warmly, and to get enough rest. Once before a tour he said, "Kinder, don't drink cold water after a concert. It is bad!"

One stormy winter day as we were leaving the railroad station in Buffalo he spied Burgin without a hat. After scolding him harshly, he sent his valet back into his train compartment to fetch a fur hat, which Burgin unhappily had to wear for the rest of the tour.

But in spite of his solicitude he could also be utterly ruthless at rehearsal. He would pick out a nasty string passage and make each stand play it alone. And if it came out well, he seemed taken aback. After one of these rehearsals there was a great run on bicarbonate of soda.

During the Koussevitzky era there used to be a great deal of discussion about his "beat." Musicians in the audience used to ask us, "How do you ever manage to start together?" He had a certain conception about beginning a piece, especially a soft beginning, that was unique. "Gentlemen, you must begin without to notice!" he would say. "The music must come from the air." And certainly there was great magic in what he tried to and did achieve. But it was nerve-wracking for us. He would begin a piece holding his arms rather high in the air, then bring them down ever so slowly, as though daring anyone to begin. I remember my first rehearsal and how frightened and confused I was. During the intermission I went to Alfred Krips, our assistant concertmaster, and asked, "How do you start? What's the secret?" And he answered, "I'm not quite sure. All I know is that when the stick starts coming down, I shut my eyes, and when I open them, everybody is playing, so I sneak in quietly."

One day when we were rehearsing Scriabin's "Poem of Ecstasy," the usual difficulties were encountered in the woodwinds as they tried to begin together without a beat, with Koussey shouting, "Gentlemen, it is awfully not togedder!" Finally he said, "I know you don't like it my beat. All right, I will give you di kind of a beat di you like." Whereupon he started again, only this time instead of lowering his arms slowly he dropped them like a shot, with no warning, no preparation. Of course nobody played. "You see, my way is better!" he said triumphantly. "It is so simple, when di stick touch di air, you come in vitout to notice!"

One of Serge Koussevitzky's great and remarkable qualities, other than his keen ears and sense of balance and sound, was his unqualified love of music, a love which was almost reverential. Few conductors I have ever known, if any, loved music qua music with such fervor. And he approached each work with such immersion, sincerity, and dedication that even an undeserving new work would emerge with force and conviction, and he was able to convey his enthusiasm to us in the orchestra.

Every concert for Koussevitzky was an event. But he reserved his greatest efforts and energies for "important" audiences. To him success in the cultural cities was more important than success (he pronounced it "*sook*-sess") in the smaller cities, which he called "the province." We were rehearsing one Monday morning for a tour to New York and Philadelphia. Suddenly Koussey stopped and said, "Gentlemen, it is good perhaps for Toledo or Cincinnati, but not for New York or Philadelphia!" These two cities were, for him, the ultimate in musical sophistication and he would drive us with demonic fury in preparation for concerts in these cities.

During my first year in the orchestra we made a visit to a number of so-called "Western" cities. The first concert was at the Museum of Art in Toledo, a beautiful concert hall in the style of a Greek amphitheatre. Koussey came out to thunderous applause, then turned around to face the orchestra. He spied me, violin held high, watching him eagerly, sitting on the edge of my seat, ready for his signal. He smiled easily, made a slight motion with his hand to me indicating that I should sit back and relax, and whispered, "Toledo!" So I sat back, and the concert began.

Such was his complete absorption in any new work that he would tolerate no adverse criticism of it at the time of preparation. After he had studied a new work and brought it to rehearsal, if it did not quite come off as he had anticipated, he felt the fault was with him and he applied himself and the orchestra with more and more energy and relentless fury to the task at hand. Once, after a rehearsal of a new work, he asked our personnel manager, Rosario Mazzeo, what he thought of the new piece and when Mazzeo, either thoughtlessly or bravely, told him he didn't like it, there was a look of scorn on Koussey's face. A few weeks later when the piece was found to have no success with audiences, Koussey said to Mazzeo, "I must ask you not to give a bad opinion while we are preparing a new work. Because while we are rehearsing, I am convinced it is the greatest in the musical literature. A few weeks later, if I ask your opinion, you may be honest, because then I might agree with you."

Such was the nature of Serge Koussevitzky's enthusiasm about people that he developed a certain failing—which even he admitted. He made rash promises which, although sincerely made, he could not always fulfill. For instance, every new man who came into the orchestra was promised the job of eventually being first in his section. And every composer was promised a performance. It is said that Koussey once told an intimate friend, "You know, I have it the weakness to make many promises, but I also have it the strength not to keep them!"

It is now more than twenty years since Serge Koussevitzky retired as Music Director of the Boston Symphony Orchestra, after having served for a quarter of a century. Inevitable changes have taken place in our orchestra since then, changes in personnel, in management, in conductors, yet the spirit of Koussevitzky still hovers over the orchestra. If I should tell you that hardly a day passes that he is not remembered and quoted, I would not be exaggerating.

Many years ago the eminent John Burk, program annotator for almost half a century for the B.S.O., wrote, "The name of Serge Koussevitzky is magic, one of those names about which legends cluster." And it is still true today. Those of us who were privileged to take part in the legend of Koussevitzky are consciously and unconsciously handing down the tradition to our younger colleagues who did not share in the era of this remarkable man.

Throughout his life Serge Koussevitzky had an adventurous, forward-looking spirit, a belief in the young composer no matter how misunderstood by the public, and during his lifetime, unlike most other conductors, he did something about his convictions. Indeed, when the history of music in the twentieth century is recorded, the name of Koussevitzky will stand out.

It was Koussevitzky who introduced to the world, through performing and publishing, the early works of Stravinsky, Prokofiev, Sibelius, Scriabin, and many others. And since the establishment in this country in 1942 of the Koussevitzky Music Foundation the musical culture of the world has been profoundly affected. Here are but a few whose works have been commissioned by the Koussevitzky Music Foundation—Stravinsky, Bartók, Martinu, Copland, Schumann, Harris, Britten, Milhaud, Villa-Lobos, Schoenberg, Fine, Kirchner, Piston. Ralph Waldo Emerson once said, "Give me insight into today, and you may have the antique and future worlds." Koussevitzky had this insight, and he was able to communicate it to others. I remember his remark when someone objected to his playing of contemporary music: "If you do not play the new, eventually you will not have the old."

The Berkshire Festival and Music Center are a perpetual monument to the vision of Koussevitzky. Because of his faith, enthusiasm, courage, and devotion to the cause of music, the Tanglewood center is today the mecca of summer musical activity in this country and indeed its influence is strongly felt throughout the musical world. Koussevitzky's legacy to the musical world has been a lasting one, not only at Tanglewood, but through the foundation, which today is ably administered by his widow, the quietly efficient and perceptive Olga Koussevitzky.

WE JOIN FORCES WITH PETRILLO

The B.S.O. was the last of the American orchestras to hold out against the musicians' union. For some sixty years, since its founding in 1881, the Boston Symphony Orchestra had resisted all attempts from without and within to have it unionized. In 1921, while Pierre Monteux was the conductor, there had been an abortive effort by the orchestra members, led by the concertmaster, the late Frederic Fradkin, but even after a number of the players "struck" a Saturday-night concert, refusing to go on the stage, the attempt failed. The program that night was quickly changed and, led by Monteux, a small Boston Symphony of chamber proportions played a concert. It is characteristic that the management of the Boston Symphony was not vindictive and invited all of the "strikers" back.

Self-portrait by Olga Koussevitzky

Fradkin, however, not only left the orchestra when the "strike" failed, but practically disappeared from the concert world. He later opened a restaurant in New York City. This was a great loss to the music world for Fradkin was a great violinist.

In those days the trustees of the orchestra were fiercely opposed to anything smacking of "organized labor." Ernest B. Dane, an oil millionaire, was chairman of the trustees and he would rather have seen the orchestra collapse than join a union. As a matter of fact, when James "Caesar" Petrillo, the president of the American Federation of Musicians, began to make things quite difficult for the orchestra by refusing to allow soloists whom he had unionized to appear with us, and these included practically everyone; then stopped us from recording with the major recording companies, which he had also unionized, and we were beginning to lose an enormous amount of income from recording royalties, Dane personally made up the deficit of about one hundred thousand dollars a year. Actually for a few years he was almost our sole benefactor, adamantly refusing to recognize the union and just as doggedly willing to pay for his obstinacy.

It was not generally known at the time, but Serge Koussevitzky himself finally instigated the proceedings which led to our joining the musicians' union. One day he telephoned his friend Carl Dreyfus, Boston newspaper publisher, and said, "Carl, I vould like it to meet this Petrillo." Dreyfus, by no means a friend of labor in general or of Petrillo in particular, told Koussey he would see what he could do. And after judicious inquiry plus a few telephone calls he got through to Petrillo, who was more than eager to meet Koussevitzky. A meeting was arranged, and on the appointed day Petrillo drove up to the Koussevitzky estate in the Berkshires in a bulletproof limousine, flanked by three bodyguards. The meeting was held in the Koussevitzky living room, and in attendance were Petrillo, his bodyguards, Koussevitzky, Carl Dreyfus, and one of the orchestra's trustees. During the course of the meeting the B.S.O. gentlemen were astounded at Petrillo's knowledge of the orchestra's affairs, financial and artistic, and all were impressed with his intelligence, candor, and reasonableness. Petrillo was ready to promise no interference in the internal affairs of the B.S.O., provided they would join his union. It was a very amicable meeting.

Shortly afterwards (Dane having died) the orchestra committee, a group of five or six players elected by the orchestra to represent it to the management, was given some hints that the trustees might consider dealing with the union, provided the members of the orchestra so desired. There followed many orchestra meetings at which the question was debated furiously. Most of the players were for the union, some were not. But when it was learned definitely that the trustees would not formally object, the men quickly voted for it. It was decided to engage as our counsel the eminent Judge Jacob Kaplan to represent us and to work out a contract with the trustees. He made such a strong impression upon the trustees that he was invited to become one of them, becoming the first Jewish trustee of the Boston Symphony Orchestra. Later they even invited a Catholic, a dear, decent, wonderful human being, Michael Kelliher, who had been fire commissioner for the city of Boston, and who was one of the pioneers in promoting good race relations in the state of Massachusetts.

There are sequels to Koussevitzky's union efforts. About three weeks after we were finally in the union, he stopped the orchestra at a rehearsal and said, "Gentlemen, I do not like your sound. Since you join the union you play like employers!" And we received a telegram from Fradkin reading, "At long last, congratulations!"

It was inevitable that the Boston Symphony join the union. There may still be some die-hards who cannot accept the fact that artists are also human beings who work for a living and have the same need for protection from exploitation as do other workers. True, it is not exploitation for profit, since a symphony orchestra is a non-profit organization, but exploitation it can be. Fortunately, the trustees were, generally, over the years, men of high integrity and were scrupulously fair in their dealings with the musicians, and salaries were always on a par with those of other orchestras; yet in certain areas we were far behind.

Before joining the union Boston Symphony musicians were enslaved to their jobs. There was no limit to the number of rehearsals or concerts each week. The conductor could, without notice, call for extra rehearsals at any time of the day or night, with the rehearsals lasting indefinitely. If nothing else, the union has "tamed" the tyrannical, whimsical, terrible-tempered conductor, who enjoyed his outbursts at the expense of the player. The musicians' union has given to musicians everywhere a sense of dignity and a measure of self-respect and has in no way lowered artistic standards. Musicians as a group have too much innate pride in themselves ever to compromise their standards.

Our present contract, arrived at after many months of negotiations, is an eminently fair one and will probably serve as a model for other orchestras to follow. Salaries, fringe benefits, and general working conditions are superior to those of other orchestras, considerations which we hope will contribute to maintaining the supremacy of the Boston Symphony.

Although we are members of the International Federation of Musicians, we in the Boston Symphony are, in practice, an autonomous organization. Unlike the custom in some other cities where the local union negotiates for the orchestra, we negotiate for ourselves. That is, through our committee of players and numerous meetings of the entire orchestra (some of them quite hilarious as a hundred emotional musicians get together) we arrive at a list of "demands." These are then presented to our own lawyer who advises and counsels us and finally they are presented to the trustees. After more meetings between our committee, trustees, and management; more meetings of the orchestra players; secret ballots; and discussions; there is a final agreement which is then taken to the local union for automatic ratification.

The International Congress of Symphony Orchestra Musicians (I.C.S.O.M.) is a comparatively recent effort of symphony and opera orchestra players to band together, within the confines of the musicians' union, for the purpose of discussing and solving their own peculiar problems. Once a year appointed delegates from each orchestra meet in a different city to discuss the welfare and artistic conditions of symphony orchestras in the United States and Canada. It is hoped that this organization will play a significant role in the future of music in America.

One of the prime considerations in future negotiations with symphony players will be that of adequate pensions. The Boston Symphony has, happily, led the way in this regard and now the other major orchestras are following suit. There was a time when a man would leave the Boston Symphony Orchestra after a lifetime of service, facing a bleak future. During my time I remember one suicide. Today a musician retires with dignity, knowing that he can live out his remaining years with some semblance of financial security. In addition to his Social Security benefits he will receive one-half the minimum Boston Symphony salary as long as he lives; and under the present system if the orchestra salaries go up, so does his pension. Our pensioners have free access to Symphony Hall and many come back for frequent visits. As one recently said, "I come back to inspect my investment. I now have one hundred and five men working for me!"

RUNNING THE B.S.O.

The Trustees

It used to be said in Boston that the Cabots spoke only to the Lowells and the Lowells spoke only to God, but the trustees of the Boston Symphony Orchestra, until recently, didn't speak to anyone. This august body, once known as the Protestant Vatican, sat on Mount Olympus, quietly dispensing its wisdom and managing the affairs of the orchestra. No one ever saw them. No one knew where or when they met. Their names appeared on every symphony program to attest the fact that they existed, yet they seemed to be mythical—until recently when, along with the emergence of the "New Boston," the trustees of the B.S.O. gradually came out of their shells and were revealed as real people. There are nineteen of them, plus four trustees emeritus, and they represent a variety of callings—several lawyers, a couple of merchants, a banker, an insurance company executive, a minister, a priest, two publishers, a judge, a United States senator, and one woman (the latter, the charming and able Mrs. James H. Perkins, a recent tradition-shattering addition). Being a trustee of the Boston Symphony Orchestra is the highest status a Bostonian can attain.

Henry B. Cabot, until very recently the chairman of the trustees, is a rare human being, forthright, honest, liberal—and loved and respected by all of the musicians. This is not the case with presidents of other orchestras, whose relationship with the players is, in some instances, one of suspicion and misunderstanding. A New England Yankee whose love of music and musicians is so great that he devoted a third of his life to the affairs of the orchestra, Henry Cabot served willingly and proudly without a cent of remuneration. As a matter of fact, he paid handsomely with both time and money for the privilege. He is urbane, quietly witty, and enormously modest. Occasionally, he has even been mildly profane. He was an iconoclast about himself and his fellow trustees. (Koussevitzky used to call them "trusties.")

Cabot recently stepped down from his position and handed over his responsibilities to a fellow Bostonian, Talcott M. Banks. With characteristic modesty Cabot announced to the members of the orchestra that his failing memory had been a prime consideration in his decision to relinquish his office. He remains, however, keenly interested in the affairs of the orchestra as a trustee emeritus.

Banks is a distinguished Boston attorney, a good amateur pianist, longtime lover of music, and a great doer in the musical affairs of the community. He is a fine gentleman, respected and loved by all who know him, and there is no reason to doubt that he will continue in the Boston tradition of sound management.

In keeping with the spirit of the times the "New Boston" symphony trustees have an ecumenical face. Henry Lee Higginson, indeed, might not recognize a Boston Symphony Board of

Trustees that now harbors in its ranks alongside a Cabot, a Jennings, a Perkins, and a Noonan, such names as Laughlin, Kennedy, Berkowitz, and Rabb.

What, then, are the duties and functions of a symphony board of trustees? Years ago their duties were quite simple. They were expected personally to make up the inevitable deficit at the end of each year, as Ernest Dane had, which they did without fanfare and without publicity, keeping these mundane affairs to themselves. The Boston Symphony was considered their private club and they were proud of their ordained heritage in keeping it so. They chose the conductor and the manager without asking or expecting outside advice and most of the time they were extraordinarily lucky in their choices, for the Boston Symphony became known as the greatest musical organization in the world. Even today, when so many other fine orchestras have sprung up in the United States, the Boston Symphony remains pre-eminent.

Conditions, however, have changed. The day of enormous fortunes being privately made and spent is gone. Today's trustees are not all men of wealth and their original function of giving money has changed to that of raising money to keep up with the ever increasing costs of maintaining an orchestra. Although the Boston Symphony still boasts that it is almost 75% self-supporting, its over-all annual budget of 5 or 6 million dollars still leaves an annual deficit of some $500,000. The private approach has had to be changed to a public one and a number of years ago an organization called "Friends of the Boston Symphony Orchestra" was formed for the express purpose of defraying the deficit. This organization has grown into one of thousands of music lovers, mainly from Greater Boston, but with branches in other cities throughout the country, who contribute each year. For their generosity they are rewarded with an annual meeting and concert in Symphony Hall, plus the privilege of attending numerous events at the Berkshire Music Center every summer. In addition, private foundations, like Ford and Rockefeller, have begun to lend their support. And it is not too unreasonable to assume that some day in the future there will be direct government support for the arts as there has been in the European countries over the centuries. Some of us have even dared to hope that some day we will have in our national government a cabinet Secretary of the Arts, whose function will be to develop the enormous talent that exists in the United States, and to bring it to the attention and enjoyment of all.

Manager

Being the manager of a symphony orchestra is quite different from being the manager of a profit-making firm. If the manager of an orchestra should show a profit, he would certainly be looked upon with suspicion. The nature of a symphony orchestra, as that of an opera company, where so many are involved in producing the finished product is such that it is impossible to break even, let alone make a profit. So it becomes one of the primary duties of a manager to keep costs down while keeping artistic standards up. The manager of a symphony orchestra, like a reluctant maiden, has to learn to say no, and to keep saying it over and over again, especially to the players.

George E. Judd, manager of the orchestra for many years, was a master of refusal. He returned to Symphony Hall for a visit a few years after his retirement and when he was seen in the corridor, four different players approached him and, from force of habit, they asked him for a raise. And, from force of habit, he refused all four!

Judd was a completely dedicated man, whose concern for the orchestra was almost religious in its fervor. He was wise, efficient, honestly shrewd, and scrupulously fair in managing the orchestra. If he sometimes seemed cold and unbending to the players, he was equally so to himself. During his many years with the orchestra he never asked for a raise in salary and indeed when the trustees voted him one, time after time, he always adamantly refused it. George Judd has been retired from the orchestra for a number of years, yet he still retains a personal and lively interest in its affairs and whenever he comes back for a visit he is greeted like a beloved father.

There are, of course, many duties and problems which beset

a symphony-orchestra manager. He must make concert schedules, arrange dates and engage soloists and guest conductors a year in advance, all with the approval or recommendation of the music director. Out-of-town concerts must be arranged, transportation problems solved, negotiations made with out-of-town managers, etc., etc.

The manager has also the task of negotiating and arranging salaries of individual orchestra players; for although the minimum salary of a player is set, only about one third of the orchestra receives the minimum. The rest, according to their position in the orchestra, seniority, and their over-all value, receive above-minimum pay, arrived at by individual bargaining.

Our present manager, Thomas D. Perry, Jr., is a soft-spoken, boyish-looking man, whose mild exterior masks an acquired stubborn toughness. He is a Yale man who broke the tradition of Harvard-bred managers for the Boston Symphony. Although not a Bostonian by birth or schooling, he has earned the respect and high regard of even our Harvard-bred trustees.

The Staff

Most people are surprised at how many people it takes to run the Boston Symphony. When I joined the orchestra I naïvely thought that the B.S.O. consisted of one hundred six musicians, a conductor, and a manager. Last year's payroll of the orchestra numbered some five hundred employees! The second floor of Symphony Hall is a maze of offices and cubbyholes peopled by librarians, the manager, assistant managers, secretaries, press officers, program editors, a personnel manager, fund raisers. The Tanglewood complex employs many additional people, some full-, some part-time. There is of course an all-year-round caretaker who lives on the grounds and oversees the physical operation of the grounds and all the various buildings. The Boston Symphony Orchestra is probably the only orchestra in the world that owns its own tractors, trucks, and other farm equipment.

The stage manager of the Boston Symphony has always occupied a unique role in the symphony family. He is as much a part of the orchestra as any player and in some respects is much more important. If a musician gets ill, he can be replaced by one of his colleagues, but if the stage manager has to miss a concert, there is a real crisis. Our stage managers have become an integral part of every concert. The late Harvey Genereux, who preceded our present stage manager, was more temperamental than any musician and actually took it upon himself to decide certain musical matters. For instance, he hated large cymbals and, on out-of-town trips, he would conveniently forget to pack them, remarking, "The small cymbals sound just as good." Before a trip he would always ask, "Are the big chimes necessary? Can't you play those notes on the bells?" Harvey also hated conductors who conducted from memory. "They give me nervous prostration," he used to say. "What if they forget!" And in many instances he would drag out the conductor's music stand and place the scores upon it, even if the conductor didn't want them. Before each of the concerts for children which I conduct, he would beg me to use the music, and each time when I didn't, he would say, "Damn fool!"

Our present stage manager, Alfred Robison, is a six-foot-five gentle giant, who watches over his brood like a mother hen. He is completely levelheaded, devoid of temperament, always cheerfully optimistic, and he does his job proudly and efficiently. He calls the members of the orchestra "my men," and when the concert goes well and there is great success, he is enormously proud. Over the years Al has also become a music critic and, by the second day's rehearsal, will predict which new piece will have success and which will "lay an egg"—and he is usually right. In the Pops repertoire his favorite is "Days of Wine and Roses," and on the evenings when we play it, he sits quietly backstage humming it to himself, swaying from side to side, a look of benign happiness on his face. On most outside Pops engagements when I am conducting, I try to make sure "Wine and Roses" is included, just for Al. So far I have never played it quite the way he thinks it should go.

Like his predecessor, Al Robison is quite concerned when

conductors conduct without a score. "Let me put them out anyway," he will say, and when I refuse, he mutters to himself, "Smarty pants," and as I walk onto the stage, his last admonition to me is "Don't blow it, now!"

One of the most unusual and extremely valuable members of the Boston Symphony until his early retirement a few years ago was Rosario Mazzeo. For many years he wore two hats in the orchestra—that of bass clarinetist and personnel manager. "Rosy" was, and still is, a man of many talents. Possessor of an inventive mind, trigger brain, and great imagination, he was not only a fine and sincere musician, but he was also an inventor, expert photographer, writer, ornithologist, and public speaker. It was Mazzeo who devised the present pension plan of the Boston Symphony Orchestra, a plan which has been studied by insurance experts and pronounced eminently sound and which has been adopted by other orchestras in the United States.

When we first played Shostakovich's Fifth Symphony and it was discovered that a low F which Shostakovich wrote for the bass clarinet did not exist on the instrument, Rosy simply devised a new bass clarinet which *did* include the F. For many years he was dissatisfied with certain clumsy fingerings on the regular clarinet, so he invented a new instrument which simplified these fingerings, and today these instruments are manufactured by the Selmer Company, bearing the name "Mazzeo System." Rosy has among his friends most of the world-famous photographers, and he himself has had numerous exhibitions of his own pictures. Still a comparatively young man, Rosario Mazzeo lives today, in his so-called retirement, with his family in a beautiful rustic home on the side of a mountain in Carmel, California, writing, teaching, bird watching, photographing—all the fruition of a plan made years ago when he joined the Boston Symphony. And some day I hope to join him out there.

Symphony Hall may be a "temple of music," but it is also a plant which requires many people to run it efficiently. On the first floor in back of the box office a suite of rooms houses the treasurer, James Brosnahan, and his staff. Here every day, and some nights, a different kind of music is made, the music of computers making payrolls and paying bills.

The superintendent's office is in the basement just behind the stage door of Symphony Hall, and further back in the basement are the quarters of carpenters, painters, electricians, and maintenance men, all employed full time by the Boston Symphony. In addition there are the occasional workers who are called in for special jobs, like removing all the seats for various purposes—recording sessions, dances, Pops concerts, etc. These men, mostly derelicts from the surrounding saloons and barrooms, are rounded up by some secret grapevine system. Whenever they are needed, usually late at night after a concert, they seem to appear, ready and eager to work for a few hours, sometimes until 2:00 or 3:00 A.M., collect their few dollars, and go back into the night.

The four men in the box office at Symphony Hall are probably the rarest such men in the United States. They are part of a profession that prides itself on insulting customers, yet the B.S.O. box-office staff, headed by Robert Carr, are polite, friendly, and even helpful. No dirty looks, no impatient snarls will you get from behind the bars at the Symphony Hall box office. Our men are well-mannered and always scrupulously pleasant.

Before each Boston Symphony concert it has long been the tradition for the manager or one of his assistants to stand in the corridor and greet the familiar subscribers, many of them by name. Back in 1881 when the orchestra began at the old Music Hall one of the requirements of Henry Lee Higginson was that the musicians were to greet the customers before the concert and to circulate in the corridors during intermission, a practice which is followed to a lesser degree even today, except that we now do it from choice. One of the pleasant traditions of the Boston Symphony is that of meeting our friends in the corridors of Symphony Hall during intermission. Indeed, one of the reasons we dislike the new Philharmonic Hall in New York is the lack of opportunity for meeting people. The orchestra seems to be barricaded backstage. During an intermission at Lincoln Center I once tried to meet a friend in the corridor and got hopelessly lost.

The Symphony Library

The music library of the Boston Symphony Orchestra on the second floor of Symphony Hall is the busiest and probably most important room in the building. It is the nerve center of all musical activity. Here surrounding our two librarians and their occasional assistants are shelves from floor to ceiling containing the orchestra's scores. On the left wall are the thousands of numbered scores of works performed during the almost ninety years of the orchestra's existence; and the right wall houses, in neatly arranged cardboard containers, the players' parts. All around the room, in seeming disarray, there are piles of music—music for next week, music for last week, music just arrived from the publisher, music about to be shipped back to the publisher, and music for the current week. Yet in all this confusion nothing ever gets lost; the players always find the right music on their stands at rehearsals and concerts.

Since there are constant additions to the library, much of the older material—music not often played—has been stored over the years in another room on the third floor of Symphony Hall directly above the library. This "second library" now contains more music than the regular library. It has been estimated that the replacement value of all of the B.S.O.'s music would be well over a hundred thousand dollars.

One cannot discuss the B.S.O. library without thinking of the late Leslie Rogers, librarian from 1912 until he died in 1953. Rogers had the most infallible musical memory of all time. It was he who installed the system of locating in a moment any score or piece of music. He even remembered all of the thousands of scores by number and all kinds of information about each piece. For instance, if a conductor should ask him about a certain composition, Leslie Rogers would say, "Oh, yes. That was first played under Nikisch in eighteen-ninety-two. It has four movements. It takes thirty-six and a half minutes, needs three flutes and piccolo, two oboes and English horn, two clarinets and bass clarinet, four horns, two trumpets, three trombones and tuba, tympani, two harps, and strings."

Rogers went through all of the scores of music played before his time and marked in each a record of performance, when and where, which conductor, and in all subsequent scores he continued these notations, adding the exact timings of each conductor. This system has been continued by our present librarian, Victor Alpert.

Rogers carried on voluminous correspondence with composers, and whenever a famous composer came to Symphony Hall, Rogers would try to talk with him about his music, with the result that many scores bear observations and admonitions delivered by the composer to Rogers. For instance, the score of Alexander Glazunov's arrangement of Chopin's "Military Polonaise" contains this remark. " 'This orchestration is rotten!' says Glazunov 'I did it when I was a young man.' LJR." We used to make some drastic cuts in Georges Enesco's "Rumanian Rhapsody" until Rogers showed them to Enesco on one of his visits to Symphony Hall. Now the score contains this admonition: "Enesco says no cuts are permissible—LJR!"

Leslie Rogers' dedication to his job was unique. His whole life revolved around "his" library. He was at his desk from morning until night, and even at home he worked on library matters. He was easygoing, slow, thorough, and very talkative. He loved to reminisce about orchestral incidents, musicians, and composers and always seemed to have time to talk, no matter how busy he was. He was a close friend of Arthur Fiedler, who depended largely on Rogers' advice and musical counsel. Occasionally when things became quite hectic in the library (their desks faced) and Leslie would begin one of his interminable stories, Arthur would say good-naturedly, "Les, start in the middle." Yet, in spite of his easygoing ways, in all the years he was at the hall no mishap ever occurred. The music was always ready for every rehearsal and concert, the parts were legible and in good order, and all of the conductors' wishes carried out.

One week in advance of each symphony concert the music is available in the library for the players to examine and take home to practice if necessary. Usually the four or five rehearsals for each program are more than sufficient for each player to learn his part technically. If, however, a particularly difficult piece is in the offing for the following week, the player can practice it ahead of time.

Even though I am a professional musician, I am constantly amazed at the ability of an orchestra to read through for the first time a thoroughly complicated and complex piece of music. Of course, the success of a first reading depends largely on the conductor, his own mastery of the music, and his technique of conveying his wishes to the orchestra. One of the many reasons for which I admire Erich Leinsdorf is his ability to do just this. He comes before an orchestra completely prepared, having worked out ahead of time the difficulties to be encountered. I remember his preparation for Benjamin Britten's "War Requiem" in its first American performance in Tanglewood. This is a large and complex work, requiring a good-sized orchestra, a smaller chamber orchestra, a large chorus, a children's choir, and three singers. Leinsdorf had worked with each group individually before the first general rehearsal and so thoroughly had he prepared every detail that that rehearsal was practically a performance. He had fitted the parts together like a fine watch.

Some conductors create a great deal of work for the librarians. In an effort to bring out the salient qualities of a score, and in their never-ending search for proper balance, they constantly "edit" scores, reinforcing here, lessening there, changing chord structures, and driving the librarians to distraction. It will probably come as a shock to some that most music written before the twentieth century is not performed exactly as the composer intended. For instance, in the music of Beethoven and Brahms, and Schubert and Schumann, the winds are almost always doubled, except in the solo passages. This is done for the sake of balance, to compensate for the larger number of strings used in our present-day orchestras, and our larger concert halls. Also, some composers, like Schumann, for instance, were not great masters of orchestration, no matter how sublime their music, and conductors, over the years, have taken the liberty of reorchestrating their scores, always with the intention of better presenting the composer's music.

Guest conductors with the B.S.O. usually send their own material with their own peculiar markings, editings, and bowings. Leopold Stokowski, for example, conducts his own version of Beethoven's Seventh Symphony with myriad changes and Stokowskian peculiarities. He prides himself on being a nonconformist, indeed boasts of it, and if he did not have his own material, there would be constant pitfalls for the players. For instance, Stoky makes sudden ritards and holds where you least expect them; he makes changes in articulation; he makes cuts; and he dislikes uniform bowing by the string players. A friend of mine once asked me after a Stokowski concert if we had had enough rehearsals. When I asked him the reason for his question, he said, "Well, none of you bowed together!" I told him that was the way Stoky wanted it. At this same concert we had played Stokowski's arrangement of Moussorgsky's music from "Boris Godunov," and the music was so badly marked up with penciled additions and corrections it was almost impossible to read. During his visit with us we played this piece a number of times and each time it was different. Sometimes his conducting indications bore no resemblance to what was in our parts. Later he told our librarian he was still, after many years, arranging it and had not yet come to a satisfactory version.

The symphony librarian's work is arduous, exacting, and time-consuming. The mere job of laying out the parts for each player and putting them into the right folders for the right concert consumes a great deal of time. He must work at least a week or two ahead in preparing for rehearsals and must have the music ready for each of the one hundred six players to look at ahead of time.

How does the librarian lay out the music for rehearsals? On a long table in the library he sets out each part, from left to right, according to the way it is written in the conductor's score —the higher instruments first, starting with the piccolo and going down to the double basses. After he has laid out each part, he goes on to the next piece, until the program is complete. He then puts each music pile into its respective folder, the folders are stacked on a wagon, and on Monday morning the wagon is wheeled to the stage where the music is distributed to each stand. This program is rehearsed all week for the regular Friday and Saturday concerts, then becomes the program for the following Tuesday and Thursday concerts, while a new program is prepared for the current week.

Each season the Boston Symphony prepares twenty-four different programs for its regular Friday and Saturday pairs of concerts. These programs are then repeated at the Tuesday and Thursday series and on the road trips. The Tanglewood concerts are also made up of music played in the winter season, with some variations. So the librarian is responsible for going over some one hundred or more works each season. The Pops season of nine weeks presents additional, different chores for the librarian. Here the program changes every night, and there are many more pieces on each concert.

Guest soloists often bring their own material (score and parts), for each has his own musical wishes about his concerto. A violinist, for example, who uses a certain kind of bowing to play a phrase that is then repeated by all the violins in the orchestra naturally wishes them to bow as he does.

A brand new work, premiered by the Boston Symphony, usually causes a great deal of excitement and extra activity in the library. I remember the first performance of the Samuel Barber Piano Concerto which was commissioned for the opening of Philharmonic Hall in Lincoln Center. The soloist was the excellent American pianist, John Browning. The orchestra parts arrived in manuscript from the publisher, in good order, except that the last movement was missing, so we rehearsed only the first two movements until the last movement came. Meanwhile, after each rehearsal Barber worked in the library with the librarian, correcting mistakes in the parts, for it seems that no matter how thoroughly a new work is proofread by the copyist and composer, rehearsals always disclose wrong notes—especially if the conductor has a keen ear. Even after a composition has finally been printed (the publisher usually waits to see what success a piece will have before he decides to print it), there are inevitable overlooked errors.

One of the important duties of a librarian is to examine all new orchestra parts as to their legibility. Occasionally the music is so badly written that it is refused performance until the publisher, or the composer, can supply better parts. It is a maxim among musicians that a clear score produces a clear performance, and vice versa; and a good librarian becomes, in a way, a watchdog for good performances.

Librarians are usually ex-players. Our present head librarian, Victor Alpert, is a fine violist who, occasionally when needed, plays in the orchestra. He is a man of extraordinary good nature and infinite patience who leads a hectic life trying to keep one step ahead of the conductor while acting as nursemaid to the musicians.

GUEST CONDUCTORS

When I first joined the Boston Symphony, a tough old piccolo player gave me this bit of philosophy: "Just as in nature every animal has its natural enemy, so in an orchestra the natural enemy of the player is the conductor. And don't ever forget it!" There are two exceptions, dead conductors and guest conductors. Every orchestra enjoys guest conductors, if only because they come and go.

One whom we hated to see go was the late Sir Thomas Beecham. Each time he came to conduct there was full attendance at all rehearsals. Nobody wanted to miss the fun. He was an eccentric with a wicked sense of humor and it seemed as though he were constantly enjoying a huge joke, on himself, on us, on the music. Frankly, I don't think Sir Thomas knew very much about music—technically. As far as I know he never performed on a musical instrument. He was unlike any professional musician I ever knew. He seemed more like a very talented and perceptive amateur. But he knew how to make music charming and convincing.

Sir Thomas Beecham by Olga Koussevitzky

At rehearsals Sir Thomas never stopped muttering either to himself or to the orchestra. There were continuous asides like "Not bad, Tommie, but make it better!" . . . "Damn fine flute playing!" . . . "Now I wonder why Sibelius wrote it like that. Stupid of him!" . . . "Bravo to you, bravo to me, but mostly bravo to Beethoven!"

The first time Sir Thomas came to our orchestra he wasn't thoroughly acquainted with our schedule. His first concert was to be on Tuesday evening, and for that concert we had three scheduled rehearsals, two on Monday, and one on Tuesday morning. We played the Tuesday concert, then assembled on the stage at 10:00 o'clock Wednesday morning for a rehearsal of the same program for the next performance. However, no Sir Thomas. At 10:45 our manager telephoned his hotel and discovered that Sir Thomas knew nothing about this rehearsal. After some urging he agreed to come to Symphony Hall. He arrived shortly before noon, shuffled to the podium, and asked, "Can anyone tell me the reason for this meeting?" There was silence. "I thought the concert went quite well last night," he went on. "Is there someone here not satisfied? Come, now; speak up!"

Boaz Piller, our contrabassoonist did speak up: "Everything was fine!"

"Well, that's good enough for me! Good day, gentlemen!" And the rehearsal was over.

On Friday afternoon we played a Beecham arrangement of a suite by Handel which had five movements. The audience began to applaud at the end of the fourth movement, at which point Sir Thomas turned around, held up his hand, and said, "Ladies and Gentlemen. Evidently you think the piece is over. I regret to inform you it is not!" And we continued to play the last movement.

On Saturday night after the concert was over, the audience kept applauding vociferously and calling Sir Thomas back to the podium. After a while he tired of it, held up his hand, and made the following statement: "Ladies and Gentlemen. When I was a very young conductor, I heard a deaf vicar in the front row say to his neighbor, 'Why is he bowing? The musicians did all the work.' So, I shall now leave, and you may applaud these gentlemen to your heart's content."

While in Boston Sir Thomas received a long-distance call at his hotel from a man in Texas. "Mistah Beecham," said the voice, "Ah'm thee president of tha English-speakin' Uneion," and Sir Thomas said, "I don't believe you!" and hung up.

Of all the guest conductors who visited us from time to time

I think the most beloved was the late dear Pierre Monteux. Actually he was not a "guest" in the home of the Boston Symphony, for he spent five seasons as regular conductor from 1919 to 1924. Why he became disassociated from the orchestra has never been clearly established, but when Serge Koussevitzky took over, he stated publicly that Monteux had left him a perfect instrument. It was Pierre Monteux who twice during his tenure had to rebuild the orchestra, first after World War I when most of the German players had gone back, and then after the abortive "strike" in 1921 when at least a third of the orchestra had left.

Pierre Monteux was a great influence upon me, both as a teacher and as a friend. He was a benign man, of tremendous musical knowledge and experience, whose approach to music, as it was to life, was humanely philosophical. His music-making was exciting because of its purity and his performances were like seasoned old wine. He was completely unhistrionic, and he was the only conductor I ever knew who could control the orchestra with a slight shrug of his shoulders, or the raising of an eyebrow, or the twitch of his walrus mustache. And he was so human.

At a performance of Stravinsky's "Rite of Spring" on a Friday afternoon in Symphony Hall, he made a mistake: he had no music in front of him, and had evidently forgotten a repeat. For a few bars there was a strange feeling in the orchestra, the feeling of a ship floundering without a captain. He quickly recovered himself, however, and brought the orchestra together and I am sure the audience was completely unaware that anything had happened. Of course these memory lapses happen with every conductor, but most of them try to cover it up. Not Monteux! When the performance was over, before he turned to bow to the audience, he pointed at himself and winked at us as though to say, "My fault, gentlemen!" And the next night as we were approaching the same place in the music, a broad smile came over his face, he again pointed to himself and made a gesture to let us know it wouldn't happen again. And of course it didn't.

Monteux's "ear," even up to his last days, was extraordinary. He could detect wrong notes in the most complicated score, and his remarkable memory enabled him to bring back to mind scores he hadn't conducted for years. Once at his school for conductors in Hancock, Maine, he was prevailed upon to conduct part of a program—he almost never conducted at the school concerts, leaving it entirely to his "pupils," some of whom were and are well-known in the symphonic field—and he chose to do an orchestral version of the Beethoven Septet. Before the rehearsal his wife said, "But, Pierre, I never heard you conduct that piece."

And he answered, "Oh, yes, I conducted it thirty-seven years ago in Paris."

"But have you studied it for the rehearsal?" she asked.

"No," he answered, "I couldn't find the score. But I remember it." And at the rehearsal he certainly did remember it, every note.

In all the years I knew him I never saw him angry or visibly upset. He had a delicious sense of humor, aimed sometimes at himself. I was driving him to rehearsal one morning in Boston. "Did you ever drive a car, Maître?" I asked.

"Oh, yes," he answered, "when I was young, I drove a car all ze time." Then he added, "You know, when you get old, you must give up some things." A few minutes later he added, "You know, Harry, when you get old, some things give *you* up!" And he chuckled.

He could also be politely sarcastic. At a rehearsal with a singer who shall be nameless and who had been consistently flat, Monteux finally stopped, turned to her, and said, "Madame, would you kindly give us your 'A!' "

Once his irrepressible wife, Doris, burst into the studio at Hancock, Maine, during a class, and shouted, "Pierre, I am leaving you and I am never coming back!" There was a hush among the orchestra and the assembled conducting students as Monteux stepped to the front of the stage, said nonchalantly, "Leave the checkbook," and went back to his seat to continue the class.

Monteux once took me on a six-hour personal tour of the opera "Carmen," an experience for which I shall be eternally grateful. We and a pianist started at 9:30 A.M. from the beginning of the opera and went through every note in every act, with him singing, gesticulating, conducting, and stopping occasionally to point out and explain the high points, the pitfalls, and the traditions of the opera he knew so well—which was original Bizet and which Guiraud interpolated after the composer's death. "Here, on this note the tenor will try to make a hold," he said. "Don't let him! Do not let anyone sing what is not written in the score—ever!" He had strong convictions about the portrayal of Carmen. "She is *not* a prostitute," he said. "She must be played seriously and with conviction as a woman to whom love means everything; and she is not afraid to die for her convictions."

We finished the first two acts at 12:30, went home for lunch, and returned to the studio at 2:30 for the last two acts. That afternoon we had a visitor—the violinist Tossy Spivakovsky, who sat there spellbound, as I was, until we finished at 5:30.

Afterwards, Monteux said to me, "Here, Harry. Take my score. I do not need it any longer. I have it all up here." And he pointed to his head. I asked him to put his name on it so I could borrow it. He obliged by writing the following: "To Harry Dickson with my true affection, Hancock 1955." When I protested that I had merely asked him to write his name, he said, "I did. Right there!"

The Monteux School for Conductors was unique at that time. There in a tiny hamlet about a hundred miles from the Canadian border Monteux made his home. There he returned periodically from his travels around the world and there he spent his summers teaching and giving of his vast musical knowledge and experience to conductors young and old—conductors just beginning, but who showed promise and talent, and conductors who had already established themselves in the musical field.

The work was strenuous, the hours long, and the Maître drove himself as hard as he did his students, sometimes as much as six or seven hours a day. Each morning the orchestra would assemble at nine in the forest studio on the Monteux grounds, with Maître already in his seat, and each assigned conductor would conduct his prepared work under the ever alert, ever benevolent, wise and often witty supervision of the master. And no one could get away with anything. If a conductor did not stop for an obvious mistake, Monteux would wave his hand. "Why did you not stop? The second oboe played an F instead of F-sharp!" If a conductor did stop, Monteux would ask, "Why did you stop?"; and if the conductor would say, "The first clarinet was wrong," he might be told, "Wrong? There was nothing wrong. You must not stop for nothing!" He loved to use American slang. "You must get on ze ball!" he would often say.

Monteux was a very simple man. He would come to each rehearsal dressed in a plaid lumber jacket and sneakers. One morning he arrived after he had been made an honorary Doctor of Music by the University of Maine. We all stood up and applauded as he came in. His first words were "Anyone who calls me 'Doctor' will be fired from the school!"

During one of his last visits to our orchestra when he was past eighty-five, we had as soloist the Russian violinist Leonid Kogan, who performed the Brahms concerto. Kogan told me that when, at the first performance, he walked out on the stage followed by Monteux and saw there was no music in front of the conductor, he almost had heart failure, but the accompaniment was the finest he had ever had.

It was during this visit that it was decided to record for R.C.A. Victor the Khatchaturian Violin Concerto with Kogan, Monteux, and the B.S.O. During one of the intermissions in the recording session Monteux was resting in an armchair in the greenroom while Kogan was furiously practicing a Bach sonata. Suddenly Monteux opened his eyes and said, "B-flat, not B-natural!" Kogan stopped, played the passage again. Again Monteux said, "No, it is a B-flat." Kogan was stunned. He called in his wife, who is also a fine violinist; they discussed it, then looked up the music to find Monteux was perfectly right. Kogan thanked him, and told him he had been playing it wrong his whole life!

For some unknown or unsaid reason Pierre Monteux was never invited to conduct the Boston Symphony during the entire twenty-five years of Koussevitzky's tenure. When Charles Munch took over, however, Monteux began a series of annual visits. He was then seventy-five and he returned each season until he was in his ninetieth year, the year of his death.

One of the warmest, most nostalgic occasions ever to take place within the Boston Symphony Orchestra was the celebration in the spring of 1955 of the eightieth birthday of Pierre Monteux. He had been invited to conduct the orchestra on his birthday with all the proceeds to go to the orchestra's pension fund and he chose a program of music he loved—all Beethoven, a program that included "Eroica" and the Fourth Piano Concerto with one of his friends and protégés, pianist Leon Fleisher, as soloist.

At my suggestion Charles Munch had written to Darius Milhaud and Igor Stravinsky asking them to compose suitable short works for the occasion. Both were lifelong friends of Monteux, who had conducted many premieres of their works. Almost immediately a score arrived from Milhaud, a short work for strings entitled "Pensee Amicale Pour Mon Ami, Pierre Monteux." From Stravinsky came a letter saying that he was very busy, but would try to find the time to write something. We waited and waited and had given up hope when, a few days before the concert, a score did arrive, not from Stravinsky but from his publisher, entitled "Birthday Prelude for Pierre Monteux," a kind of parody on "Happy Birthday." Along with the manuscript came a bill for a performance fee! Our librarian, however, called the publisher and shamed him into waiving the fee for this unusual occasion. It was decided that both of these works would be played as a surprise for Monteux after the intermission of the concert and Munch would conduct them. So, a few days before the arrival of Monteux, we rehearsed them in secret session.

The performance was a gala affair. Over the stage was a huge garland of flowers spelling out the letters "PM" and the numbers "80." Across the front of the stage there were green wreaths and white flowers and each member of the orchestra wore a white

Pierre Monteux by Olga Koussevitzky

carnation in his lapel. (The violinists and violists wore them on their right lapels so as not to crush them with their instruments.) At the end of the intermission Monteux came out accompanied by Munch and the chairman of our trustees, Henry Cabot. The latter read citations from the Governors of Maine and Massachusetts and a few of many messages and telegrams which had arrived from all parts of the world, including those from the Queen of Belgium, the Presidents of France and the United States, and Chief Justice Earl Warren. After Cabot left the stage, Monteux was invited to sit down while Munch conducted the two birthday pieces. (Incidentally the "Birthday Prelude" of Stravinsky is now published and finds its way to occasional concert performances, with a suitable fee to Stravinsky. The piece by Milhaud rests in the archives of the Boston Symphony library.)

After the concert there was a supper party at a Back Bay hotel attended by the entire orchestra and friends and pupils of Monteux. At the head table in addition to Mr. and Mrs. Monteux and Mr. Munch were people whose association with Monteux had begun when he was the permanent conductor of the Boston Symphony. Among these was Dr. Archibald Davison, the eminent conductor of the Harvard Glee Club, which had first performed with the Boston Symphony many years back under the baton of Pierre Monteux. Also sitting at the head table was Richard Burgin, concertmaster of the B.S.O., who had been engaged by Monteux back in 1920. In Burgin's remarks he spoke of his indebtedness to Pierre Monteux for bringing him to Boston and for having changed the course of his life.

Perhaps the most moving speech of the whole evening was that of another head-table guest, Roland Hayes, the world-renowned tenor. Hayes was the first Negro artist ever to appear with a symphony orchestra in America, and it was under the insistent sponsorship of Pierre Monteux, back in 1923. I remember Hayes' words well: "Pierre Monteux gave me my chance at a time when it was not fashionable to give a Negro a chance and because of his courage, others of my race have followed into the concert world."

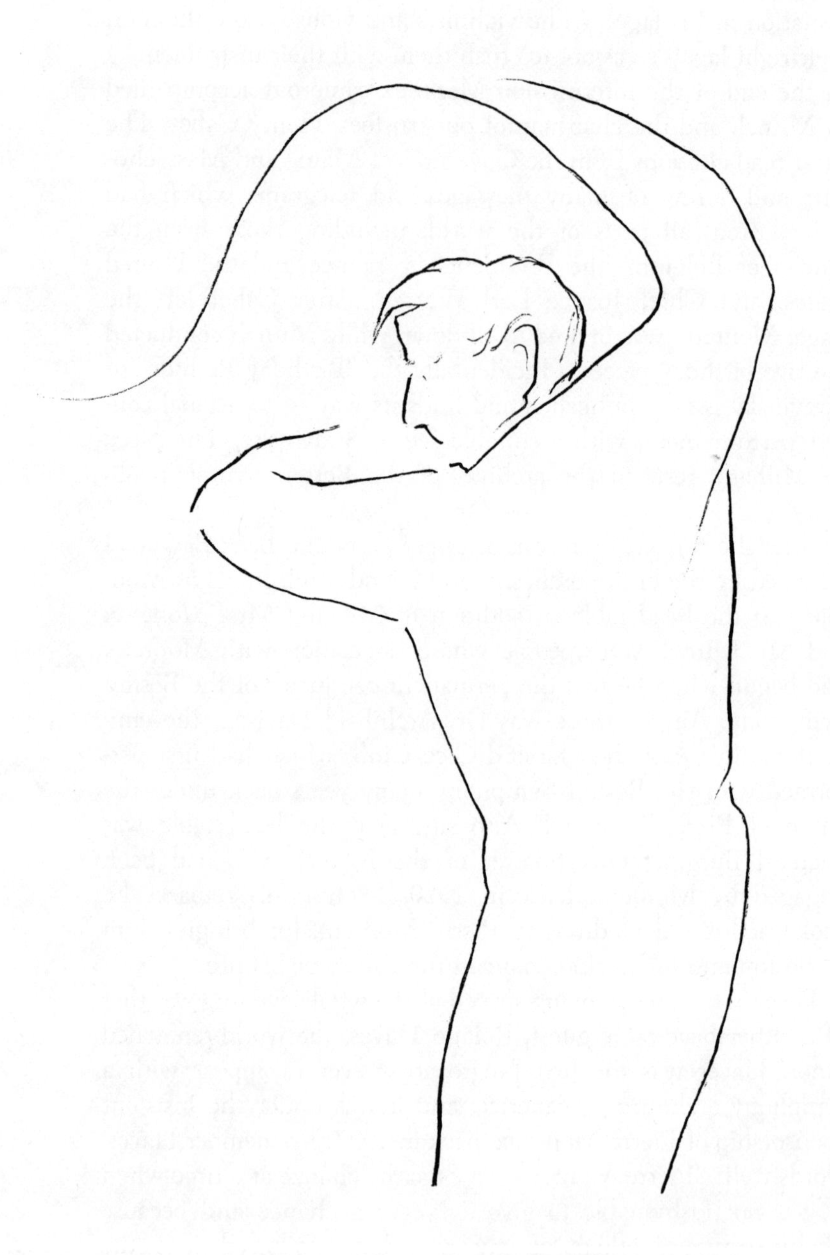

Charles Munch by Olga Koussevitzky

After supper there was a short "concert" in honor of the birthday guest. One of the members of the orchestra, Jacobus Langendoen, had written a "biographical homage" to Monteux. It was a very humorous chamber-music piece written for twenty players, all of whom had been engaged by Monteux when he was the conductor of the B.S.O., and it contained musical references to Monteux's life, all cleverly interspersed with strains of "Happy Birthday." Following this a small group of strings presented "a serenade by an unknown composer." This was one of Pierre Monteux's youthful transgressions, a piece he wrote at the age of eighteen and which lay hidden in a pile of music in a closet in Maine, which, with Mrs. Monteux's help I had unearthed. We had had the parts copied from the score and rehearsed it surreptitiously. Before we presented it, I made an announcement saying that we had discovered this work by an unknown composer and wished to test the infallible memory of our guest. After we started to play it, a broad grin came over Monteux's face, he turned to his wife and asked, "Where did they ever find that?" then sat back to listen, as he said later, "in embarrassment." When the piece was over, he stood up and said, "Ladies and gentlemen, I think you will agree that after hearing this piece we should let the composer remain unknown."

My greatest satisfaction of the entire affair came the following summer when I attended the Monteux school. Mr. Monteux took me aside and said, "Harry, I want to thank you for my birthday party. I will pay you back some day by making one for you on your eightieth." I thanked him and answered, "Maître, I doubt if I will make it, but I am sure you will!"

We of the Boston Symphony were privileged to spend one more birthday party with Pierre Monteux, his eighty-fifth, when he again conducted a gala concert for our pension fund. After that he came back to conduct each season until the year of his death, 1964, when he was eighty-nine.

The late Fritz Reiner was one of the last of the conductor-tyrants. During his lifetime he must have fired at least three times as many musicians as he had hired. Indeed, at his funeral it is said he fired two of his pallbearers! Yet we looked forward with a certain amount of curiosity to his first guest appearance with us. We had heard about his nastiness, his cold sarcasm, his cruelty to musicians, and we were ready for him. Since he was only a guest, we were prepared to take no nonsense. When he was introduced by the manager, there was polite applause. He made the usual remarks about how happy he was to be with us and then asked for the Strauss Domestic Symphony. He began to conduct with that tiny characteristic beat that was his trademark, sitting back on his high stool, and for the next ten minutes peered over the top of his half-glasses at the entire orchestra while he conducted without stopping and without saying a word. He then rapped his baton on the stand. The orchestra stopped and waited expectantly. "Gentlemen," he said, "I am enjoying myself immensely!" And for the rest of that week all was milk and honey. No conductor was ever kinder to the orchestra. After all we had heard about him it was almost a disappointment.

Reiner was one of the most sophisticated of all the conductors. His approach to music was unemotional, matter-of-fact, and so utterly professional that it seemed almost cynical. Indeed, at some of the rehearsals he seemed completely detached from the music. Yet one had the feeling that he knew exactly what he was doing. His attitude was not unlike that of Paul Hindemith, who once told me he never listened to his own music if he could help it. He knew how it should sound, so why listen!

One of the tragedies of our generation was the untimely death of Guido Cantelli, who was killed in a plane accident as he was flying from Rome to New York to conduct the Philharmonic. Cantelli was just at the beginning of what would have been a great career. A protégé of Toscanini, he had all the requirements of a conductor, musical talent, a handsome demeanor, an air of great sensitivity, and an aura of untouchability. He was still quite young, but he had already learned from his master Toscanini how to cause incidents at rehearsals and had already been warned by the union about his behavior. Even during his first appearance with our orchestra he walked off the stage during the rehearsal in a temperamental huff. He soon returned, however.

Before one of our public rehearsals I went into his room to

ask the order of the rehearsal. Rosario Mazzeo, our personnel manager, was in the room as was Mrs. Cantelli. "Mister Cantelli," Mazzeo said, "this is Mister Dickson. He tells the audience what we are going to rehearse, so would you give him the order of the rehearsal?"

"Certainly," answered Cantelli, "but please, Mazzeo, don't call me 'Mister.' I am 'Maestro.'" And at this point his wife began a tirade at him that lasted until I left the room. Since it was in Italian, I did not understand it clearly, but Mazzeo translated it later: "Such a fool, such a child, such an imbecile! You are in America now and one doesn't behave that way!"

The next day the blunt but soft-spoken Laning Humphrey of the Symphony Hall publicity staff had the occasion to talk with Cantelli and he said to him, "You know, *Mister* Cantelli, the title 'Mister' is an honored one in this country. Even the President is called 'Mister.' On the other hand, I have a barber who is called 'Maestro' by all his clients."

No discussion of Boston Symphony guest conductors would be complete without mentioning one of the greatest, Danny Kaye! And while the reader's eyebrows are raised, let him read on. After Kaye's first appearance as a conductor with the Boston Symphony the erudite music critic of *The Christian Science Monitor* wrote as follows: "By any musical standards whatsoever Danny Kaye is a great conductor." When Kaye appeared with the London Philharmonic Orchestra, one of the critics said, "Not since the appearance of Giulini in the Verdi 'Requiem' has the London Philharmonic played with such passion and fire as it did under Danny Kaye!"

My many years in the Boston Symphony have brought me many rewards, but none greater than my friendship with Danny Kaye. A number of years ago he walked into the tuning room backstage at Symphony Hall after a Friday-afternoon concert. Having heard that he had "conducted" at a benefit concert in Philadelphia, I asked him when he would conduct our orchestra. "Any time you ask me," he said. So I took him up to the conductor's room, introduced him to Munch and Perry, our manager, and by the time he left the room Danny and the man-

Danny Kaye by Olga Koussevitzky

agement had concluded an agreement for him to conduct a pension-fund concert in three weeks.

As we walked out, Kaye asked me my name. Then he said, "Well, Harry, you've just gotten me into a big mess. I've never conducted more than ten minutes of music in my whole life!" So for the next three weeks we had daily "conducting" lessons in Danny's hotel suite between shows. (He was doing his own show every day at the Colonial Theatre.) A record player was brought into his room, we armed ourselves with lots and lots of records, and Danny went to work learning some symphonic repertoire. Since he doesn't read a note of music, of course everything had to be done by rote. On the night of the concert he conducted over two hours, a program which included Rossini, Tchaikovsky, Strauss, and Wagner. Since then he has added Ravel, Beethoven, and Verdi.

It is impossible to describe what goes on at a Danny Kaye concert. He is a great natural talent and has a fantastic ear and musical memory. I sat with the late Dimitri Mitropoulos one morning while Danny was rehearsing the New York Philharmonic and Mitropoulos suddenly turned to me and said, "You know, this isn't funny. This man is a great conductor!" And one evening at dinner the French conductor and composer Jean Martinon said to Danny, "You have a great advantage over us conductors. We spend a good deal of our lives with our heads in the score, then we try to get away from the score in order to make our music alive and spontaneous. You never had to put your head in a score, so you do everything naturally and spontaneously and don't have to go through our agonies. And your music-making is therefore more alive and natural!" William Steinberg, when asked about conductors, always maintains that, everything considered, Danny Kaye is still the best!

Dimitri Mitropoulos was a fine, decent, altruistic man, loved and respected by musicians. He commanded the attention of his players because they respected him as a musician and loved him as a man. Such was his selflessness that he gave away most of his possessions and all of his money, mainly to needy musicians and music students.

Dimitri Mitropoulos by Olga Koussevitzky

His first appearance in the United States was in 1936 when Koussevitzky invited him to come to Boston to conduct the Boston Symphony. He created a sensation, so much so it was said that Koussevitzky resented it. "*Personne* knew him before my invitation, and now he made it such a success!" said Koussevitzky to a friend, as though somehow he had been betrayed.

What an impression he made upon the orchestra at that first rehearsal! He was one of the first conductors after Toscanini to display a fabulous memory. Not only did he have no scores at the rehearsal, but he knew the rehearsal numbers in the music and what page each musician was playing on. He also called each player by name! Afterwards, when he was asked how he did it, he said, "It is really nothing at all. Anyone can learn to do it. As for the musicians' names I consider it the conductor's duty to know his players, so on the train I memorized their names. It is really nothing." The world lost a great conductor when Dimitri Mitropoulos died of a heart attack on November 2, 1960.

In 1944 Koussevitzky invited Andre Kostelanetz to conduct a pair of concerts and many eyebrows were raised among the musicians and the audience. Although Kostelanetz had received a well-rounded classical education, having attended the St. Petersburg Conservatory in his native Russia and having served as assistant conductor of the Imperial Opera in that city, his reputation in this country was based upon performances of semi-classical and popular music "souped up" in typical Kostelanetz arrangements, mostly over the radio. Especially he was known for his Coca-Cola commercials.

His appearance with our orchestra was a revelation. None of us was prepared to work with a serious, highly intelligent, extremely musical, modest, first-class musician. Yet that is what we found Kostelanetz to be. His program, consisting of a Kabalevsky overture, a piece by the American Paul Creston, a suite from Stravinsky's "Firebird," and four arias with his wife, Lily Pons, as soloist, was altogether delightful and was conducted with consummate artistry.

We had expected a certain amount of showmanship from Kostelanetz, but, on the contrary, he conducted with a quiet dignity and self-effacement, applying himself only to making good music. An example of his sincerity was his not using the scores at rehearsal (to save time), but having them on the podium at the concerts. This is a procedure usually reversed by most conductors.

In talking with him after the concert I asked him why he didn't have a symphony orchestra of his own. "You find me one," he said, "and I'll give up everything to conduct it—even Coca-Cola!"

One of the most beloved of all conductors was Charles Munch. Blessed with handsome features and a benevolent smile he was the idol of all the ladies. They swooned as he approached the podium. He was impulsive, unpredictable in his tempos, unmeticulous in technical or musical detail, yet had the power of bringing an audience to a frenzy of excitement. Unlike most conductors he hated to rehearse, thereby endearing himself to orchestra musicians. After rehearsing a few bars of a piece he would invariably stop and say, "Pas necessaire," and go on to something else.

His performances were highly subjective affairs where he relied almost entirely upon his feelings of the moment, with the result that his readings varied greatly from one performance to the next. He was said to have remarked at one time that a conductor who knew ahead of time exactly how fast or slow a piece would go was no conductor. For us musicians this concept made for interesting if sometimes nerve-wracking concerts. No one could take anything for granted at a Munch performance, for things were seldom played exactly as they were rehearsed; and timings of symphonies could vary as much as ten minutes from one performance to the next. (Because of these qualities he was called both an amateur and a great artist.) He was a generous, warmhearted person who loved his musicians more than his audience.

There was an incident during his tenure as Music Director of the Boston Symphony Orchestra (after Koussevitzky, from

1949 to 1962) when one of our colleagues in the orchestra became severely ill and had to spend many months in the hospital. This was before our present hospitalization insurance plan was in effect and the man became quite financially drained. The members of the orchestra decided to help defray the enormous hospital costs and Munch insisted on joining us in this venture. He contributed a sum so substantial that I went to him and told him we could not accept it. He was furious with me. "I am an old man," he said. "What better use do I have for my money than helping a colleague!"

If Koussevitzky had no sense of humor, Charles Munch had a well-developed one. At an orchestra party one night I imitated some conductors and soloists, their gestures, mannerisms, etc. Remembering my unfortunate experience with Koussevitzky, I omitted Munch from my parodies, but he insisted that I imitate him. I protested that I had a wife and family to support, but he assured me that he would not fire me; so I did. (I had had a few drinks.) He guffawed loudly and we remained good friends.

A few weeks after the incident we had as guest soloist the English pianist Solomon. During the rehearsal of the Brahms D Minor Piano Concerto Munch looked at the soloist, a broad grin came over his face, and he looked down in my direction and winked. "Dickson," he said, "please come to my room at intermission." I wondered, as did the rest of the orchestra, what I had done to be so summoned, and I was a little uneasy. When the concerto was finished, I went up to Munch's room, knocked on the door, and found him engaged in conversation with George Judd, the manager of the orchestra. When he saw me, he excused himself from Judd, took me into his dressing room, and asked, "Can you see the face of the pianist? Such faces he makes when he plays! Try to study him. He will be your best imitation!" And with that he dismissed me and went back to his conversation with the manager.

One of the greatest legitimate musical sensations of our time is the ubiquitous, the flamboyant, the iconoclastic, the gifted, the most talked-about musician of our time, Leonard Bernstein. He grew up with the Boston Symphony Orchestra, was one of

Leonard Bernstein by Olga Koussevitzky

Koussevitzky's first and most beloved pupils at the Berkshire Music Center, and from the beginning of his career was recognized as an enormous talent.

In 1949, after Serge Koussevitzky had spent twenty-five years as music director of the orchestra and felt he could not continue to shoulder this great burden, he suggested to the trustees that he be given two assistants, Eleazar deCarvalho and Leonard Bernstein. The trustees felt that they were both too young and inexperienced, and Koussevitzky was turned down. He threatened resignation and the trustees, true to their patrician nonchalance, accepted it and within a few weeks had a successor, Charles Munch. Bernstein, meanwhile, went on to become conductor of the New York Philharmonic, the most successful of all his predecessors.

If Bernstein's talent extends in all directions, so does his personality and almost anything one could say about him would be true. Although his admirers are legion (among them this humble musician), he also has many detractors, yet everything he does is convincing and vital. And Leonard Bernstein remains one of our great cultural assets. He is also intelligent, articulate, generous, boyishly enthusiastic, and a most sympathetic human being.

The name of Stokowski has been well-known in and out of musical circles for many years, and during his prime more was written about him than any other conductor. For twenty-six years, from 1912 to 1938, he was the conductor of the Philadelphia Orchestra, an ensemble which he built singlehandedly into one of the greats of the world. His dynamic personality, his unpredictable flamboyance, and his complete and studious disregard for conventionality plus his scandalous personal life kept him in the public eye most of the time and perhaps that is why he was never invited to conduct the Boston Symphony until late in his life. Not until March, 1964, when Stokowski was almost eighty-three, did he come to conduct us.

I had never played under him, and I, as well as my colleagues, had looked forward to the experience. When he appeared on the podium for the first rehearsal, we rose and applauded and he made a short speech of the usual clichés. His conducting turned out to be rather perfunctory with very few stops for corrections and when he did stop, his observations were quite inconsequential. Most of his rehearsing all week consisted of starting a piece or movement and going through it without stops. His occasional corrections or observations were directed mainly to the percussion players, with some admonitions to the strings to use more bow and never, never to play uniformly. "Free bowing" was his expression—which is a fancy way of saying "no bowing." (Stoky has the strange conviction that uniform bowing by the strings stifles self-expression.) I got the distinct impression that he was unconcerned with the intellectual or inner emotional content of the music or even the technical aspect. Effect was what he was after, effect upon the audience. And there were those in the audience who told me after the concert that they had never heard the orchestra play so freely and with such fiery abandon.

Many stories have been told about Stoky's unorthodox and unpredictable behavior, but we saw none of it in Boston. We had heard, for instance, that while he was in Philadelphia he would often lecture the audience on their concert manners and he had been known to stop the orchestra in the middle of a movement and glare at a member of the audience who had the audacity to leave before the piece was over. At a concert for young people he once brought onto the stage of the Academy of Music an entire menagerie, including a baby elephant to illustrate Saint-Saëns' "Animal Carnival." If he played a new composition and it was not received enthusiastically, he would lecture the audience on their ignorance, then repeat the piece. Once, after he had played one of his own Bach transcriptions, a lady came back after the concert to tell him how much she liked it, and when she asked him if Bach were still composing, he looked her straight in the eye and said, "Madame, he has been decomposing for many years!"

One hot and sticky August Sunday afternoon at Tanglewood the musicians had been given permission to play in their shirtsleeves, but Stokowski walked onstage attired in a heavy black cutaway coat, afternoon trousers, pearl-gray vest, Windsor tie, and high wing collar. He looked like a character from the pages of Charles Dickens.

Before a public rehearsal at Tanglewood I asked Stokowski what I could say about him to the audience. "You may say anything you like," he said, "as long as it is true."

Remembering his well-publicized escapades with Greta Garbo and his former wife, Gloria Vanderbilt, I facetiously asked, "How about some scandal? The audience would love that."

"Go right ahead," he answered, "but be sure it is true." And then with a wicked gleam in his eye he added, "It probably is, you know!"

An unsuccessful conductor once made the cynical remark that the two prime requisites for success are a rich wife and a good tailor; and if three of the Boston Symphony's recent conductors have met those requirements, perhaps it is only a coincidence. The most sartorially resplendent of all was Serge Koussevitzky. His clothes were made in Paris and draped him with patrician elegance. During his later years, after he became an American citizen, he began to patronize native craftsmanship and had some of his clothes made by a superb tailor in Brockton, Massachusetts, William Tonis. Tonis, a fine amateur flutist, music lover, and great admirer of Koussevitzky, gave his all, above and beyond the call of duty, and his resultant efforts pleased Koussevitzky no end.

(Speaking of clothes reminds me of the story told to me by a former first cellist of the Boston Symphony, Joseph Malkin. A tailor in Vienna was famous for his wonderful trousers and it was said that no other tailor in the world could duplicate his cut and fit. He was a very slow and meticulous workman and could not be hurried and one who ordered a pair of trousers from him had to be prepared to wait for a long time. Fritz Kreisler once came into his shop and ordered a pair of afternoon trousers. After being fitted he told the tailor that he was leaving for concerts in Germany and Paris and would be back in four weeks. He returned then and was told his trousers were not ready; he returned two weeks later and they were still not ready; then again a short time later; and this went on and on for months. Finally the trousers were ready. Kreisler tried them on and even though he was immensely pleased, he said to the tailor, "The good Lord took six days to create the entire world and you took six months to make a pair of pants!" And the tailor answered philosophically, "Yes, but look at the world—and now look at my pants!")

Compared to the elegance of Koussevitzky, Richard Burgin's complete disregard for outward appearances was striking. Whenever he conducted the orchestra, either as associate or later as guest conductor, he looked as though he was convinced that people came to hear, not to see. Often Richard appeared as if he had taken his suit out of a drawer after it had been rolled up for a week. On one occasion he forgot his white tie, which was fortunately pointed out to him by a stagehand just as he was about to go on stage.

Because they do not often wear formal clothes, composers who come to conduct their own works sometimes have embarrassing minor mishaps. When the American composer Gardner Read came to conduct his own composition, the tie-backs on his vest came undone during the concert and while they were flapping, he tried to retrieve them and conduct at the same time. At the end he was a nervous wreck. On another occasion Lukas Foss, the composer and now conductor of the Buffalo Philharmonic, had been invited by Koussevitzky to conduct his own composition, "Recordare," at a Carnegie Hall concert. He came out, took a bow, gave the downbeat, and his tie fell off. During the playing of his piece he kept periodically staring at the tie, careful not to step on it as it lay at his feet, and at the end, just before turning around to bow, he swooped down and retrieved it.

If an exception proves the rule that conductors are natural enemies of players, Sir John Barbirolli is certainly that exception. Each time he has appeared with us in Boston he has gained our admiration and great affection. His music-making, as well as his manner, is warm, friendly, intelligent, and highly ethical. Sir John had the misfortune to appear upon the American scene as conductor of the New York Philharmonic immediately following Arturo Toscanini and no one in the world could have had a tougher assignment. Yet he remained as conductor of the Philharmonic from 1936 to 1943. Since then he has been the conductor of the Hallé Orchestra in Manchester, England, the Houston Symphony in this country, and has appeared as guest conductor of most of the orchestras of the world.

Sir John's appearance belies his speech. He is dark, slight, with sensitive Latin features and fiery eyes, but speaks with a British accent which is, of course, quite natural since he was born in London. His manner at rehearsals is kindly and warm, without any suggestion of airs or pomposity. Often he will come down from the podium, take the cello of the first player (he began as a cellist), and demonstrate a musical passage. Once when we applauded such a demonstration, he shrugged and said, "Gentlemen, you are very kind, but I haven't practiced in a long time." Occasionally he would stop to deliver an anecdote. While he was conductor of the New York Philharmonic the first oboist was the legendary character Labatti, the man who took no nonsense from conductors. It was he who once said to Otto Klemperer, after he had taken fifteen minutes to explain the hidden meaning of a phrase while nobody listened, "Mister Klemp, you talka too much!" Labatti had made some lucky financial investments and when someone asked him if he ever got nervous, he answered, "Me nervous? With hundred thousand dollars in da bank?" Sir John told us that Labatti once asked him, "Maestro, what are we gonna play now? Schub?" Barbirolli, unable to resist, replied, "No, we play Moz."

R.C.A. Victor advertises the Boston Symphony as "the aristocrat of orchestras" and we of the old guard are fiercely proud of that designation. Each performance is, for us, a challenge to do our best regardless of what we think of the conductor and if he is a man of great knowledge, inspiration, and communicative powers, the performance is that much greater. I know of no single instance when a member of the orchestra has consciously tried to sabotage the conductor, even though there have been some occasions when the temptation was almost overpowering. I remember vividly one such occasion during an Esplanade concert with a guest conductor, who shall be nameless, when the orchestra's frustration over the impossible tempo taken by the conductor resulted in near rebellion. It was in the first movement of the Beethoven "Eroica," which the conductor insisted on beating "in one" like a fast waltz. At first the orchestra tried to hold him back, but when this seemed fruitless and he seemed oblivious to our efforts, flailing away with his baton faster and faster, the orchestra, as one man, seemed suddenly to decide to follow him. The movement threatened to get completely out of hand when the conductor realized something was wrong. He then tried to slow down, but by this time the orchestra was so wound up that no matter how he tried there was no stopping us, and the movement ended in a mad furious blur. When it was over, he looked sheepishly at the concertmaster, who studiously avoided his gaze.

On another occasion after much pleading, the late Charles O'Connell, recording producer for R.C.A. Pops records, was allowed by Arthur Fiedler to "conduct" part of a Pops concert. In the "Russian Sailors' Dance" he started on the wrong beat and stayed with it throughout the entire piece. It was difficult for us to stay together while avoiding his gestures, but somehow we did, except that at the end we finished a beat ahead of him, followed by a resounding swish of the baton in the empty air.

B.S.O. "FIRSTS"

In December, 1944, Béla Bartók came to Symphony Hall to hear the first performance of his Concerto for Orchestra, which had been commissioned by Serge Koussevitzky. We had rehearsed the piece for a number of days and Koussey was tremendously excited about it for, as always, it was "di greatest vork since Beethoven."

Finally, two days before the premiere, as we assembled for our regular morning rehearsal, a little white-haired, frail, esthetic-looking man appeared in the balcony overlooking the stage. Koussevitzky introduced Béla Bartók and we launched into the first movement of the concerto. But not for long. Almost immediately there was a cry from the balcony: "No, no! It is too fast!" Koussevitzky reddened a bit, stopped the orchestra, and started again. This time we played about two bars. Then again from the balcony: "No, no! It is too loud!" Koussevitzky reddened a bit more, we stopped and started again.

We got through about four bars before there was another cry from the meek little man in the balcony. This time Koussey tried to ignore the outburst and gamely continued, playing the first page or so accompanied by varied groans and shrieks from above. Finally we stopped and Koussey said, "Please, Mister Bartók, you vill take it a pincil and paper and write it your observations and ve vill talk during di intermission." At which point Bartók took out of his pocket a long piece of paper and pencil and for the entire duration of the composition wrote furiously and continuously.

It must be remembered that for Serge Koussevitzky to take orders from anybody was impossible, even from a composer about his own work, for when Koussevitzky played a composition for the first time he "possessed" it. It became, in his mind, his own, as though he had written it himself.

When we finished playing the Bartók piece, we dutifully applauded the composer. Koussevitzky turned to Bartók to find him still writing furiously and not even acknowledging the applause. An intermission was called and Bartók was still writing up there in the balcony. After the intermission he was gone, and Koussevitzky said to us, "Gentlemen, I have it a talk with Bartók and he say, 'Everything is fine!' "

A no-nonsense composer was Paul Hindemith. Koussey soon found out that he could get nowhere with him. If Hindemith wrote "pp," it meant just that, and if he wrote "allegro," it meant that too, and he would allow no deviations from his written directions. After a while Koussey stopped playing Hindemith.

In the 1930's and 40's we played a great deal of Aaron Copland's music, many first performances, much to the consternation of one of the Russian violinists in the orchestra who not only disliked Copland's music, but stoutly maintained that all of it sounded the same. When we first rehearsed "Appalachian Spring," he calmly said to me, "I see Copland has composed a new title!"

A man who has made a tremendous impact upon musical composition in the twentieth century is Igor Stravinsky, now in his late eighties, and some of us remember his dynamic appearances with us as conductor of his own works, some for the first time anywhere. Stravinsky was not a great conductor; indeed, he often got lost in his own music. To some, it appeared that he was absolutely devoid of a sense of humor. Yet, in 1957 the B.S.O. performed for the first time Stravinsky's "Canticum Sacrum," for chorus and orchestra and when the parts arrived, it was discovered that there were neither violins nor cellos in the score. Since it was an unprecedented occurrence that the violinists and cellists would be able to "rest out" a piece, there was great rejoicing in these ranks and the following telegram was sent to Stravinsky: "Heartiest congratulations for your superb orchestration of the 'Canticum Sacrum.'" [signed] The violinists and cellists of the Boston Symphony Orchestra." And almost immediately a telegram came back: "Glad you like my orchestration. Too bad the others don't share your enthusiasm."

As a conductor Stravinsky presented a strange picture. Short in stature, wiry, and dapper, he always came to rehearsals with a white turkish towel draped over his shoulders, which, as the rehearsal progressed and he began to perspire profusely, he would pull up over his head like a prize fighter. He conducted with angular, ungraceful motions and accompanied all his gestures with rhythmic grunts. He said very little, stopping only for technical corrections, and his unsmiling, expressionless face displayed no emotion whatsoever. If his music was abstract, so was his method of conducting. There was about him, however, an aura of classic greatness, and we knew we were in the presence of a master.

The first American performance of Stravinsky's "Le Sacre du Printemps" took place in Symphony Hall in 1924, with Pierre Monteux conducting the Boston Symphony. The premiere had occurred some ten years earlier in Paris, also with Monteux conducting, at which performance there was the most scandalous demonstration ever witnessed in a concert hall. It is said that fist fights broke out in the hall among the audience. There were hisses and boos and catcalls and Stravinsky had to leave the hall

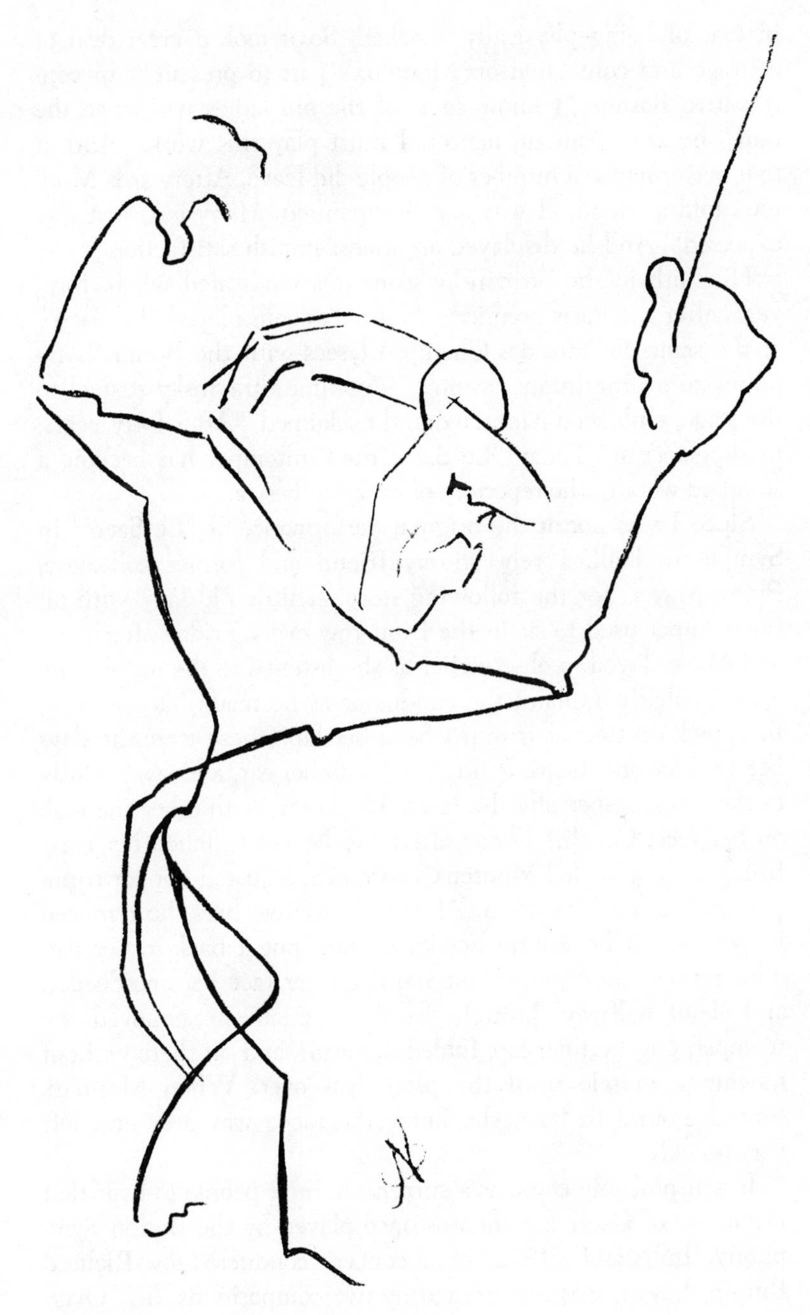

Igor Stravinsky by Olga Koussevitzky

in fear of being physically attacked. So it took a great deal of courage and conviction on Monteux's part to present it in conservative Boston. "I know some of the old ladies will leave the hall," he said, "but no matter. I must play this work." And at that performance a number of people did leave. Afterwards Monteux told a friend, "I was not disappointed. Many left, just as I expected!" And he displayed an almost impish satisfaction.

His faith in the Stravinsky score was vindicated when, forty years after the Paris premiere, Monteux again played "Le Sacre" at the same Théatre des Champs-Elysées with the Boston Symphony to a tumultuous ovation. This time Stravinsky rushed to the stage, embraced Monteux, and exclaimed, "After forty years, finally success!" Today "Le Sacre du Printemps" has become a standard work in the repertory of every orchestra.

Since I was not at the original performance of "Le Sacre" in Symphony Hall, I rely on my friend and former colleague, Pierre Mayer, for the following story. A little old lady with an ear trumpet used to sit in the front row every Friday afternoon, and Mayer loved to observe her as she listened to the music. She would politely applaud the conductor as he made his entrance, then pick up the ear trumpet from her lap (these were the days before electronic hearing aids), put it to her ear, and sway gently to the music, especially the music she knew, with a beatific look on her face. On this Friday afternoon Mayer watched her carefully. She applauded Monteux's entrance, adjusted her ear trumpet, and sat back to listen. After the first few bars she removed it, pounded it briskly on her knee, then put it back to her ear. This time as she listened, the scowl on her face became deeper, and about halfway through the first section she removed the trumpet, put it on her lap, folded her arms, and sat there without moving a muscle until the piece was over. When Monteux turned around to bow, she knew the piece was over and left very quickly.

It will probably come as a surprise to most people to hear that the music of Oscar Levant was once played by the Boston Symphony. In March, 1942, at a concert conducted by Richard Burgin, Levant was represented by two compositions, his "Overture" and "Dirge in Memory of George Gershwin." I do not remember the music, but I do remember meeting Levant after the performance in the conductor's room. After I was introduced to him and muttered the usual "bravo," he said to me, "Can I talk to you for a minute?" We went into the adjoining dressing room. I couldn't imagine what he wanted. We had never even met before. He came to the point immediately. "What did you think of those pieces?" he asked; and before I could answer, he continued, "Pretty lousy, huh?" I protested that one should never ask an orchestra musician's opinion about a new piece of music, for he is too involved in the mechanics of playing it, and besides he cannot hear the over-all effect of the piece. "Then it was lousy?" he insisted.

"If you really want a humble opinion," I said, "I thought the 'Dirge' was over-orchestrated. It seems to be a simple piece dressed up in too fancy clothes."

"Well," he said, "I wrote it for a very small orchestra, but blew it up for this performance. Pretty lousy, huh? Anyway, thanks a lot." And that ended our conversation and brief acquaintance.

Walter Piston has been aptly called the court composer for the Boston Symphony. Although born in Maine, he has been a resident of Boston most of his life and is considered one of our prime cultural assets. For many years Professor of Music at Harvard University, his career as a composer has been closely tied to the Boston Symphony. His debut as composer took place in Symphony Hall in 1928 when Dr. Koussevitzky introduced his "Symphonic Piece"; and many of his later works were first played by our orchestra.

Piston is a gentle, laconic, soft-spoken, unpretentious man, down-to-earth and quietly witty. In his music he is an expert craftsman and although he has experimented with all kinds of musical "systems," including the twelve-tone Schoenberg method, he remains basically conservative. He once told me, after listening to us play an ultramodern, crazy piece of music, that no matter how he tried to write like that, it always came out Piston. "When I hear music like that," he said, "I feel like Papa Haydn!"

The Boston Symphony always enjoys the first reading of a new Piston work. First, his score and parts are always meticulously legible and he knows the instruments so well that his music is always playable and fun to play—especially his wonderful witty scherzos. Over the years, from Koussevitzky to Munch to Leinsdorf, we have become accustomed to seeing Piston on the first balcony during rehearsals of a premiere, where he discreetly and quietly makes suggestions to the conductor. Never have we seen an outburst of temperament or impatience on his part. He sits there benignly with his score, enjoying what he hears. Occasionally, he quietly shakes his head, but never raises his voice. During one rehearsal when Koussevitzky took the tempo slower than Piston had indicated, he said afterwards, "It wasn't as I wrote it, but it was beautiful just the same!"

Our first performance of Benjamin Britten's "Spring Symphony," under Koussevitzky, evoked a great crisis in the orchestra. At one point the score called for a "cow horn," and the sophisticated Koussevitzky, ignorant of pastoral life, asked the brass players for suggestions on how to produce the sound of a cow. Our tuba player came up with a small baritone horn. "No," said Koussey, "it not sound like a cow!" He asked one of the trumpet players to play the part. "Mine dear," he exclaimed, "have you ever heard a cow with a vibrato!" Finally, the trumpet player produced a bass trumpet which made a weird sound not unlike that of a distant animal in distress. "That is just right," said Koussey, and the matter was settled. Each time we performed the piece he would gaze in the direction of the "cow horn" and smile contentedly.

If orchestra musicians are, on the whole, reactionary about new music, and usually dislike it, they are also patient and long-suffering and will prod through anything put before them, to the best of their ability, no matter how little they may understand it. I know of no orchestra that has ever rebelled over performing a new work. Grumbling there is aplenty, but rebellion, no. The inherent discipline and self-respect in every professional musician compels him to give his best, even though he may be convinced the composer is a lunatic.

Occasionally a new composition will come along with demands upon our instruments for which we are completely untrained and present us with maddening problems which cannot be solved. We recently played for the first time in the United States a new work by the eminent Argentinian composer, Alberto Ginastera, in which the violins at a certain point in the "music" were asked to play the "highest note possible on the instrument." There is no highest note on a stringed instrument that can be identified as a note. If the violinist puts his finger high enough on the string he will produce a squeak, but the squeak of each player will differ from that of the other. When I examined the score I thought, "The composer is merely striving for the weird effect of an indeterminately pitched high sound" until I noticed that he had asked for half the players to tune their instruments a quarter-tone higher than the rest! I would defy anyone, including the composer, to detect the difference in the resultant bedlam sound. The very last "note" of the piece is written in an indeterminate way with the instruction, "Play the lowest note on the instrument," and I could not help thinking, "Doesn't the composer know what the lowest note on a violin is?"

Much of the music of today is music of sound effects and composers have found it expedient to issue instructions to the players, instructions which have no bearing on the players' musical ability. In his piece called "Symphonic Studies" Ginastera has included with each musician's part two pages of explanations of his unique symbols. I am sure half of the players did not bother to read these explanations and I am equally sure it made no difference in the performance, for each of the nine movements had a boring sameness of ineffectual "effects," with or without the explanations. Many of us in the orchestra were convinced that Danny Kaye's unwritten symphony, in which he leads the orchestra through a series of spontaneous improvisations and sound effects, has as much meaning. At least it has the virtue of being funny! Yet, I must keep an open mind, remembering what critics of the past have said about works which are today considered classics. Perhaps my grandchildren will understand and even enjoy this kind of music and will look upon me patronizingly as an old fogy.

After every performance of a new work we are invariably asked, "Did you like that?" and the questioner is usually hostile. How can we answer, when often even after many rehearsals we simply don't understand it? After the first rehearsal of a work by his friend Darius Milhaud, Monteux admitted to me that he could not understand it, but "we must play it anyway, and perhaps we will learn to understand it." Musicians' reactions to a new composition are not necessarily pertinent to its value. We are concerned with technical problems; we don't get balanced over-all reproduction of the score; and unless each musician takes the time to study the entire composition from the score (which usually is not available), he is just as much in the dark as is the listener. Some new works we enjoy playing, if only because they present unaccustomed challenges and problems, which bring satisfaction when they are solved.

Orchestra musicians have general preferences as to the music they enjoy playing. I think it would be agreed that the music of Mozart is the most difficult, because it is exposed, pure, meticulous. No musician can play Mozart without perspiring. So we must put Mozart at the head of the list of music musicians hate to play. Next comes Schubert, in which the strings hardly ever get a bar's rest. Beethoven is the most satisfying although physically exhausting; Brahms a little less so. Baroque music (Bach, Handel, Vivaldi) presents no problems and is most enjoyable, while the difficult-sounding bombastic music of Berlioz, Tchaikovsky, Dvorák, Rimski-Korsakov, Wagner, and Richard Strauss is easy.

When I first joined the orchestra, I used to practice diligently the pages of impossible Wagner passages, only to discover they were not heard. Wagner himself proclaimed to the frustrated string players that all he wanted was an effect, and did not expect anyone to play all the notes. When the music of Richard Strauss first appeared, its technical demands were far greater than those of any previous composer, yet today its technical virtuosity is taken for granted and even lesser orchestras play it with a high degree of skill. The sophisticated music of Debussy and Ravel is always fun to play, especially when the conductor has imagination. (Under Charles Munch no two performances were ever alike.) Most orchestra players enjoy the music of Stravinsky, with its unexpected rhythmic devices.

As for present-day ultramodern and avant-garde music, there are probably the same percentages of protagonists and detractors among musicians as there are within the audience. I used to know an old musician who was a member of the Boston Symphony when it was founded in 1881. When asked if they played modern music, he answered, "Oh, yes—Brahms, Dvorák, Tchaikovsky—we played lots of modern music in those days!" And he went on to say that at the first reading rehearsal of Brahms' Fourth Symphony there was general agreement that Brahms had become senile!

MAKING RECORDS AND A BROADCAST

One of the important sources of income for the B.S.O. is that of recordings, and this activity is looked upon with great favor by the members of the orchestra, not only for its gain to the orchestra but for its financial benefit to each one of the players. Periodically Symphony Hall is transformed, according to R.C.A. Victor specifications, into a recording studio by our stage crew for the nerve-wracking but interesting job of making records. The well-known fine acoustics of the hall make it ideal for this purpose, yet certain modifications are necessary. In the days before the advent of the present sophisticated stereo, binaural and trinaural recordings, we used to record from the stage in our regular seating arrangement.

Nowadays, however, most of our recordings are done on the floor of the auditorium. All the seats are removed except the back rows. Curtains are suspended along the rear of the hall from ceiling to floor, the balconies are draped with heavy cloth, large plywood boards extending from the floor to the first balcony are put up on the right and left sides of the orchestra, and to the rear of the orchestra there is another plywood screen. The orchestra is thus practically enclosed on three sides. Strings of lights are suspended across both second balconies. Some eighteen or twenty microphones are placed throughout the orchestra on high adjustable metal stands. Next to the conductor's podium is another shorter stand to which is attached a small red electric light bulb, the signal that the tape machines are rolling. There is also a telephone for private conversation with the control room, situated on the second floor in the Ancient Instrument Room at Symphony Hall. This room, temporarily converted for the purpose, houses a control desk, two tape machines, and three speakers, plus a microphone and telephone for conversation with the stage. All of this equipment is, of course, brought by R.C.A. Victor from New York each time we record.

During the actual recording and testing the "producer," the man in charge of the recording, sits at the control desk with stop watch and score. He is a combination musician and sound engineer and the finished product is, to a large degree, his responsibility. For many years the R.C.A. men in charge of Boston Symphony and Pops recordings have been men who seem to have infinite wisdom and profound musical knowledge, which they dispense more or less discreetly to the conductor. During the recording sessions I keep thinking of the difficulties they would encounter with Serge Koussevitzky were he alive and recording today, for he always looked upon record making as a necessary evil and considered recording apparatus as infernal machines. He would brook absolutely no interference with his own music-making, and would allow no suggestions from the control room.

Once when Charles O'Connell was in charge of producing Boston Symphony recordings for R.C.A. Victor, he made the mistake of suggesting that the clarinets play a little louder. Koussevitzky exploded. "Mister AhCahnell," he said, "you vill take care from di apparaht and I vill take care di artistical t'ings!" O'Connell never made that mistake again.

Recording on tape as we do today is a far cry from the old wax-acetate days when recordings had to be made in four-and-a-half- to five-minute chunks, the maximum time allowed on a wax record. Since there was no splicing, if a mistake occurred during any part of the segment, even at the very end, the whole side had to be done again. Once when we were recording Debussy's "La Mer" with Koussevitzky, at the end of one segment there was a high trumpet note which, due to nervousness and unbearable tension, the player would invariably crack. The music had been segmented by Koussevitzky and O'Connell ahead of time and there was no other way to finish this particular side except with the high trumpet note. After numerous "takes," each of which was spoiled by the trumpet note, everyone was becoming more and more tense. Finally it came out beautifully. Our trumpeter beamed silently, waiting for the red light to go out, and Koussevitzky, in his great exuberance, blurted out, "Thanks to God!" The red light went out and O'Connell came running onto the stage with tears in his eyes. "Thanks to God!" was on the record. It had to be done all over again.

Today recording techniques are, in a way, much simpler than they used to be. We can now record an entire movement of a symphony without stopping and if anything goes wrong, we can go back to the mistake itself, correct it, and have it spliced into the recording. Engineers have developed the technique of splicing to a fine art. In works with narration it is no longer necessary for the narrator even to appear at the recording session. The music and narration are made separately and later spliced together. We have been told that not only can an entire chord be excised or transplanted, but even a single note can be added or taken out of a chord.

A "Live" B.S.O. Broadcast with Koussey

Years ago when radio was still in its infancy, N.B.C. decided to broadcast a series of rehearsals with Koussevitzky and the

Boston Symphony. These were live, unedited, unrehearsed rehearsals, enlivened by Koussey's carefully prepared remarks to the orchestra. At certain predesignated points in the music he would stop and make corrections and observations, usually preceded by "Gentlemen, it is awfully not togedder!" (After one of these broadcasts one of the players went home and was greeted by his five-year-old son: "Daddy, why can't you play together?")

At one of these broadcasts we were rehearsing the Concerto for Orchestra in D of Philipp Emanuel Bach. After we had played a few bars of the slow movement, a solo for the English horn, Koussevitzky rapped on his stand, the orchestra stopped, and he addressed his remarks to the English horn soloist, Louis Speyer, "Mister Speyer," he said, "you know vot Saint Paul said it?" We all looked at each other in disbelief. Did he say "Saint Paul?" And what did St. Paul have to do with us, or the Boston Symphony, or with Louis Speyer? We listened carefully as Koussey proceeded. "Saint Paul said it, 'Ven you talk to your children, talk to dem vit music from your heart,' and so must you play dis music from Bach, vit music in your heart!" Koussey beamed as he spoke these fervent words and we continued rehearsing. At the end of the broadcast, just before he dismissed the orchestra, he turned to Burgin, our concertmaster and said, "Nu, Richard! How you like vot Saint Paul said it?"

(Note: After diligent research on the life and writings of Saint Paul, I have not found this quotation.)

THE B.S.O. ON TOUR

Perhaps not too many people have ever thought about the problems of logistics connected with a tour by the Boston Symphony in this country and abroad. Moving some one hundred six musicians and eleven and a half tons of instruments and baggage from one city to another and one country to another requires careful planning. There are wardrobe trunks, trunkfuls of music, music stands, a conductor's podium, nine big bass trunks, eleven cello trunks, two harps, five or six kettledrums, bass drums, snare drums, cymbals, xylophones, assorted other percussion instruments, all kinds of brass and woodwind instruments, and specially lined cases for the more delicate violins and violas. Before each trip the librarian makes sure he has packed the music not only for all the scheduled programs in the various cities, but for emergencies. Once in Japan when almost fifty per cent of the orchestra became ill, Charles Munch had to change the program and conduct a chamber orchestra.

The Beethoven "Eroica" symphony is carried automatically on all tours of the orchestra, to be played in case of the death of a famous person. When F.D.R. died in April, 1945, we got word on the train to Philadelphia and that night we played a memorial concert for the late President, including, of course, the Funeral March of the "Eroica." As a matter of fact, this Beethoven Third Symphony has become a kind of symbol of sadness for us in the orchestra. The day J.F.K. was assassinated we had had word just before our Friday afternoon concert that he had been shot; how seriously we did not know until, after the first piece on the program, our two librarians suddenly appeared on the stage to hand out the music for the "Eroica." Then we knew.

During the past few years when most of our travel is by air there has arisen a new problem, that of plane mishap. Now, on all our travels the full complement of the orchestra never flies on the same plane. The orchestra is divided into two sections. The strings, the woodwinds, the brass, and the percussion are evenly divided, so that if something happened to one plane the rest could still give a concert. (A comforting thought to our wives and families!)

Out-of-town trips used to be much more exciting than they are today. Somehow or other, when we left Boston in our own Pullman train and, in some cases, lived on that train for two weeks, it was more glamorous than today's quick plane hops. Gone are those happy days when our wives would see us off at

South Station in Boston and wave to us as our special train would pull out with banners flying, a big BSO ON TOUR sign at the rear of the train. Within minutes the poker game would start in the club car, a friendly game that would end the next morning in Buffalo, with a few winners, and a few minus their week's salary.

A wonderful spirit of camaraderie existed on the trains. On my very first trip I happened to have a lower berth and when I offered it to an older colleague in exchange for his upper, he said, "No, I would like to be fair about it. Let us toss a coin." I told him it wasn't necessary to toss a coin. He could have it anyway. But he insisted. So we tossed, and I won.

"Look," I said, "I won, but you can still have it."

"No," he said, "let's toss again!" I left him standing in the aisle as I crawled up into the upper berth.

Those were the days when I discovered what an enormously large family I came from, for in almost every city a different relative showed up, sometimes with unpredictable results. We arrived in Cleveland one wintry afternoon, and on the station platform I saw a man walking up and down, looking at a photograph in his hand, and shouting "Dickson, Dickson?" I stopped him, and he said, "Come with me." Then it dawned on me! This was the husband of my mother's cousin, a cousin my mother had not seen since their early days in Russia some thirty years ago. My mother had sent her a photograph of me and so I went home with my newly found second-cousin-in-law to a tempestuous welcome. My mother's cousin was a fat, good-natured Jewish mother who, upon seeing me, burst into tears. "Just like your mother you look. I would know you anywhere!" she sobbed. "Come, I will make you something to eat." When I protested that I wasn't hungry, she said, "At least a glass of tea and cake you'll have!" I had the tea and cake. Then came a jolting pronouncement. "You will stay at least a couple of weeks!" No, I told her, that was impossible. We were playing in Cleveland that night and were leaving for Pittsburgh in the morning. "I won't let you go," she said. "You come here once in a lifetime and you think I will let you go in one day?"

"But I can't," I said. "I am here with the B.S.O., not on a pleasure trip."

Then she asked, "How many are there in the orchestra?"

"A hundred and six," I answered.

"So," she said, "they certainly don't need you!"

"They may not need me," I said, "but I need them!" It took a bit of arguing, but the next morning she released me, not, however, before providing me with a lunch to "take with." It mattered not that the train ride from Cleveland took but a couple of hours. I had to take the lunch. And I remember vividly distributing among my hungrier colleagues chunks of roast chicken and gefilte fish.

The first concert of every trip is the most trying—the night we discover what we forgot to bring. One night our tuba player opened his trunk only to find he had forgotten to pack his instrument. Some frantic telephone calls produced a tuba, a greatly appreciated loan from the local symphony player. On the first night as we dress in front of our enormous wardrobe trunks (each houses four people), there is a constant exchange—a pair of black socks for a white tie, a pair of trousers for a white vest, cuff links for a collar button. On one of my early tours with the orchestra I discovered I had left my white bow ties at home. A colleague loaned me one of his, the kind you have to tie yourself, which I couldn't do. When I asked him if he could tie it for me, he said, "Sure. But you'll have to lie down on the floor."

"Why?" I asked.

"Well," he said, "I used to help my father, who is an undertaker and this is the only way I know how."

"No thanks," I said, and that night I learned how to make a bow tie!

Adrift with Shostakovich

Another time in Cleveland while the orchestra was introducing the then brand-new Fifth Symphony of Shostakovich we gave a performance that can only be described as a catastrophe. In the first movement Lukas Foss, who was playing a rhythmic passage on the piano, suddenly found he was not quite together with Koussevitzky's beat and no matter how he tried he couldn't seem to get on the track. Georges Mager, our first trumpeter, knew that he should get a cue from Koussey for his low trumpet notes, but Koussey was too busy trying to correct the pianist. So Mager took it upon himself to play anyway. Not for long, though. Koussey waved him away. Our second trumpeter, Marcel Lafosse, tried to save the day by playing his part quite loudly and each time he tried he was also waved away by Koussey. Unfortunately the strings had nothing to play during this battle of alternate blasts and silences and for a fleeting and painful moment it seemed that we would have to stop. Our concertmaster, Richard Burgin, saved the day by beginning to play, all alone, on the next page and we all followed him right to the bitter end of the movement. During the cacophony I glanced up at Koussey and thought he would have an apoplectic stroke. His face was purple!

The next morning the erudite music critics of Cleveland described a wonderful performance of the Shostakovich Fifth Symphony—and perhaps it was!

A number of years ago, when the orchestra traveled by Pullman, we played a concert at Constitution Hall in Washington and were on our way back to New York for more concerts. George Zazofsky had just recently acquired a beautiful Guadagnini violin which he would not entrust to the regular orchestra instrument trunks so he carried it with him everywhere. On this particular night he had left the violin in his upper berth while he went to the club car before the train started. After the train left Washington he went back to his berth to discover his violin was gone. Someone had come aboard while the train was in the station, as we later found out, and stolen it. It was an expensive violin and, although insured, Zazofsky was heartbroken. About two weeks later the violin was discovered by the police in a pawnshop in Alexandria, Virginia. The pawnbroker had given the thief five dollars, not for the violin, which he thought was worthless, but for the new case!

Zazofsky was notified that he would have to come to the police station in Alexandria to redeem his violin. So he immediately left for Alexandria, arrived at the police station fearing that the instrument had been damaged. The police captain handed him the violin case, which Zazofsky quickly opened and found, to his great relief, that the violin had not been harmed. He thanked the captain, and was about to be on his way when the captain said, "Hold on! How do I know you're really a musician?" So Zazofsky played "Danny Boy" for the captain and a group of police officers in that police station in Alexandria, the most enthusiastic and appreciative audience an artist could ask for, according to Zazofsky.

The Russian Trip

In 1956 the Boston Symphony made its second European trip, a six-week tour climaxed by five concerts in the Soviet Union. The tour began with two concerts in Ireland, one in Cork, and one in Dublin. It was our first visit to Ireland and we enjoyed every minute of it. We had arrived in Cork two days before the concert and so were able to see a bit of the beautiful countryside. Some of us took an all-day bus trip, visiting some of the quaint towns and villages that dot the southwestern part of Ireland—Limerick, Kinsale, and Blarney. (Of course we kissed the stone at Blarney Castle.)

The bus was filled with Irish people who were the friendliest, happiest people I had ever met. There were frequent stops for a "wee bit of refreshment," and I realized this was a part of a way of life. There must be more saloons per capita in Ireland than anywhere else in the world. Yet they must know how to hold it, for in the four days we spent in Ireland I never saw anyone intoxicated.

The orchestra had been brought to Ireland through the efforts of Michael Kelliher, who had recently become our first Irish-American trustee. So proud was he, that he just had to take the Boston Symphony to County Cork, where he was born. At the concert he made a speech in which he said that he had left Cork as a poor boy many years ago and now was proud to bring back to his native city the great Boston Symphony Orchestra. He became so emotional in front of all his relatives (there must have been a thousand Kellihers in the audience) that he almost broke down.

The concert was a great success and the audience most appreciative. We were the first American orchestra to play there, but we found out later that the County Cork Musical Society had brought many other European orchestras to their city, including the Vienna Philharmonic, the Berlin Philharmonic, the London Symphony, and the Leningrad Philharmonic.

As I walked through the streets of Cork the next day, I was particularly intrigued by a sign on a shop window—Hyman Nathan, Tailor. I couldn't resist going in. An old man greeted me. "Are you Hyman Nathan?" I asked.

"That I am," he answered in a thick brogue. When I told him I was with the Boston Symphony, he exclaimed, "The blessin's o' God upon ye! Sit down. I enjoyed your concert very much." Like most Irishmen he seemed to have plenty of time for talking, so we had a very pleasant half hour. When I asked him if he had been born in Ireland, he said, "Oh, no, I was born in Poland. I came here when I was a young man." He had been an itinerant peddler, traveling all through Europe and had settled in Cork.

"Why Cork?" I asked.

He was silent for a moment, then blurted out, "I'll be God-damned, I never thought about it before!" He insisted that I go home to dinner with him to meet his wife and large family of children and grandchildren, but I had to refuse because we were leaving that day for Dublin. His last words were "Too bad. Mama makes the best bloody gefilte fish you ever ate!"

We were the first Western orchestra ever to play in Russia, and the excitement generated throughout the United States, to say nothing of that among the members of the orchestra, was high. Before our departure we were briefed by a member of the State Department on the cultural and diplomatic importance of our visit to the Soviet Union and advised on our behavior while in that country. We were asked not to engage in politics, ours or theirs, not to denigrate their system nor boast of ours, to be as discreet as possible in our conversation with the Russians, and to remember at all times that we were guests of their government. We were also asked not to photograph planes, airports, and bridges.

Our last concert before entering Russia took place in Helsinki, Finland. The next morning we assembled at the airport in Helsinki and were told that we would be flown to Leningrad in small Russian planes, each taking about thirty passengers. Before take-off I surreptitiously aimed my camera out of the airport window and took a picture of the first Russian plane I had ever seen. Any minute I expected to be apprehended, but nobody saw me. Later we found out from the Russian officials themselves that it was permissible.

After we boarded our plane I unconsciously, from force of habit, fumbled for my seat belt. There was only one strap and so I called the buxom stewardess to complain about it. "Oh," she said, "don't worry. It will be a smooth flight. Not necessary seat belts!" Then I asked her if we could smoke. "Why not?" she asked. "Look in cockpit. Pilot is smoking!" Just then the co-pilot jumped into the plane, pulled the door shut, and before he made it to the cockpit we were already moving. It was the quickest take-off I had ever seen. We taxied to the end of the runway, turned without stopping, and in about ten seconds were airborne. The flight from Helsinki to Leningrad, over the Finnish Gulf, took about an hour. Our descent to the Leningrad airport was even more hair-raising than our take-off. There was no gradual descent. The plane seemed to plummet from the sky to the ground with no nonsense. After a quick taxi to the airport building the co-pilot ran from the cockpit before the plane had even come to a stop, and opened the door.

We were met by a rather large delegation from the Ministry of Culture, plus a few musicians from the Leningrad Philharmonic Orchestra, with flowers and extremely friendly greetings. We had to wait for the other planes to arrive before there was an official greeting. Meanwhile we made small talk, in English with those who understood, and through an interpreter with others. One lady from the delegation said, "I notice you have cameras. Why don't you take pictures?" We told her we had been advised not to take pictures of airports or planes. "Nonsense!" she said. "Please take all you wish."

Finally, when the other planes arrived and the entire orchestra was assembled on the field, the Minister of Culture made a welcoming speech in Russian and her words were interpreted to us in English. Then, we were driven in buses to the Europa Hotel, situated across the street from Philharmonic Hall where we were to play.

After being assigned to our rooms we were asked to go to the dining room for breakfast. This was a sumptuous repast including eggs, caviar, many varieties of smoked fish, black and white bread, butter and cheese, and a hot beverage that was called coffee but bore little resemblance to what we know as coffee. It was a brew of *some* coffee, but more chicory, and hot milk, all cooked together, and served in a glass. I think I was the only one who enjoyed it, because it reminded me of my younger days when my mother used to serve this "coffee." The restaurant, we were told, was at our disposal any time of day or night, and everything was free except wines and liquors. After breakfast the orchestra was taken on a tour of the city of Leningrad, accompanied by three guides who pointed out with great pride the interesting aspects of their city.

That night, since there was no concert, the orchestra was taken to a Russian theatre to see a play. Having other plans, I did not go and was later told that I had missed a very boring evening. No one understood the actors, the plot, or what was going on, but all had to sit through to the bitter end. I, on the other hand, had spent the evening at the home of a Russian family—a family of father, mother, and twenty-year-old son. The father was a professor of philosophy at Leningrad University, the son a student of languages at the same university, whose hobby was collecting Louis Armstrong records, and who spoke English well enough to act as interpreter. The father had an insatiable desire for information about the United States and during our conversation, which went on into the early hours of the morning,

I realized that I was engaging in just the kind of political talk we were asked to avoid. Yet I couldn't resist. He told me he was not a member of the Communist Party, yet he believed that eventually the whole world would become communist, and how could I not agree with him. "But," I said, "what about freedom and personal liberty? Do you really believe that the people of the world want to be enslaved? Do you think the entire world will become a planet of terror, like your country is now?"

"Oh," he answered, "we don't have communism here yet. We have a dictatorship of the proletariat, which is necessary until we can someday have a true communistic society. Up until now we have unfortunately had bad people at the head of our government, but now things will be better." By this time we had discovered that we both could continue the conversation in broken Yiddish, so we dispensed with the son's translation. Then he asked me what we in America thought of Khrushchev. I knew the Russian word "groobyan" (vulgarian) and blurted it out. He looked at his son, then furtively around the room, and said, "I, too!"

After the first Leningrad concert we went back to the hotel, and I was talking to Thomas Perry, our manager, when the Minister of Culture came into the lobby followed by three men, one carrying a paper bag. She approached Perry and asked him to follow her into an anteroom. I went along too and was dumbfounded to see one of the men empty the contents of the paper bag on a table. Thousands of rubles poured out! This, Perry was told, was our fee for the concerts. He stuffed the money back into the paper bag and thanked the Minister. The next day we were each given hundreds of rubles to spend as we pleased. Since it was forbidden to take any of it out of the country, there was a mad dash for the department stores. I still have a black fur hat and six silver tea-glass holders.

Our three concerts in Leningrad and two in Moscow were fantastic successes, with people surrounding us after each concert and either staring or saying some words in English, occasionally asking if we knew a relative in Chicago. One man approached me after the concert in Moscow and asked if I knew his cousins,

Phil and Leopold Spitalny. A theatre conductor, he had not been in touch with his cousins for years and when I offered to send them his greetings, he agreed, but "please ask them not to write to me."

After our last concert in Russia we were tendered a "State" banquet in the Metropole Hotel in Moscow. This was a gala affair with lots of borsch and vodka and many speeches. Dmitri Kabalevsky, who speaks English quite well, was the toastmaster, and he called on many of his colleagues for speeches, among them Shostakovich, Khatchaturian, David Oistrakh, Rostropovich, Kogan, Kondrashin, and many others. I remember particularly the words of Khatchaturian: "Today I heard sounds from an orchestra which I never thought possible, and now that I have heard you and what you can do I must write something especially for you!"

That night, or rather the next morning, we began our exodus from Russia—again in shifts. The first group left for the airport at 2:30 A.M., the rest following in one-hour intervals. We were on our way to Prague, with a stopover in Vilna. Our plane came down in Vilna at about 8:00 A.M. and we were ushered into the airport restaurant for breakfast, which, we discovered, consisted of roast chicken and cucumbers! I inquired of the waitress if this was the standard breakfast. "Well," she answered, "we never know what time planes will arrive. If you arrive at dinnertime, you would get the same meal."

Since that 1956 visit of the Boston Symphony to Russia many other American and European orchestras have toured there and, we are told, conditions have improved greatly.

Since 1887 the B.S.O. has been giving regular subscription concerts in New York. One week out of each month from November to March the orchestra goes on tour, playing in New York, Brooklyn, and some surrounding cities and towns and these trips have become a familiar way of life for all of us. Although there are some die-hard individualists in the orchestra who prefer to stay away from their colleagues on these trips, most of the members live in hotels in the vicinity of Carnegie Hall, even though our two regular subscription series have now moved uptown to Lincoln Center and Carnegie Hall has taken a back seat.

Many of the orchestra members eat regularly in a small restaurant on Seventh Avenue, aptly called the "Carnegie Delicatessen." Over the years the "small" restaurant has become rather posh, with constantly improving décor. The proprietor, however, has remained simple, kindly, and friendly. He greets each of us every time we arrive with a "Hello, Boston! Welcome to New York!" and although he is acquainted with the entire orchestra, he knows not one name nor what instrument each plays. And he has never been to a concert.

Some time ago, on one of our New York trips we were told he had suffered a heart attack and was in the hospital. The following season he was back, greeting us more profusely than ever. "I must tell you how much pleasure you gave to me in the hospital," he said to us as we came in. "I used to watch your television broadcasts and it was like meeting all my old friends. I recognized all of you. There was the lean corned beef, there was the double pastrami, there was the matzo-ball soup. I knew you like my own brothers!"

Playing in different halls on our tours has made each of us sensitive to acoustics and every member of the orchestra fancies himself an expert. Whenever we play in a new hall there are inevitable discussions and comparisons. A hall to a musician is like a new suit. No matter how good it may look to others, if it doesn't *feel* right, it isn't right. A stage must be comfortable for the players. They must be able to hear their neighbors clearly and without distortion and if a hall "feels" good to the musician, it will sound well to the audience. Musicians have favorites, and usually they are the old friends—Carnegie Hall in New York, the Academy of Music in Philadelphia, Orchestra Hall in Chicago. Our own Symphony Hall is, of course, the best place for us since we are so used to it. But other orchestras constantly praise its qualities, too. Sound engineers have proclaimed it ideal for recording, and I remember Stravinsky's enthusiasm when, after conducting a concert, he said, "This is surely the finest concert hall in the world!"

Each concert hall has its own peculiar qualities. One is very live, another just as dead, one is mellow, the other brittle and harsh, and there seem to be many reasons for this variation of standards. We musicians are apt to over-simplify the problem. Why can't they just follow the specifications of the good hall and build the new ones the same way? Well, it's not so simple. Architects understandably want to express themselves with new ideas, new concepts of building structures, and in some cases, with radical designs—and they don't always see eye to eye with the acoustical engineers, who have definite standards of sound measurement, reverberation, quality, etc. The catastrophic acoustics of Philharmonic Hall at Lincoln Center when it was first opened were the result, we are told, of unwillingness on the part of the architects to follow the exact specifications of the acoustical experts—specifications of design and material. When we played there during opening week, it was disastrous to us. We could not hear each other, the balance was bad, and we had the feeling of playing in a large open field. Such was the protest from critics and public that the entire stage had to be torn up, the seats in the auditorium had to be redesigned, changes had to be made in the walls and ceiling, and the "mistake" cost thousands of dollars. And, as of this writing, we understand even further changes are contemplated.

New halls are like new instruments. They must be "played in," and many good concert halls have become even better as they have grown older. Also, an orchestra learns to adjust itself to each hall. Occasionally when we are to play in a brand new hall and there is time, the conductor will call an "acoustical rehearsal" in the hall before the performance. When we played in the new Powell Symphony Hall in St. Louis, there was no time for a prior acoustical rehearsal and this was unfortunate, because we were completely unprepared for the overpowering blast of sound that was created when we played the opening chord of the "Meistersinger" prelude. As the program progressed, however, the orchestra unconsciously tempered its dynamic range to suit the hall and by the end of the concert we were "giving less but enjoying it more." This new concert hall in St. Louis, beautifully remodeled from an old movie theatre, will, with some minor acoustical adjustments and "playing in," be one of the finest in the United States.

Occasionally an auditorium does not live up to its expectations. We had always heard that the Concertgebouw in Amsterdam was one of the finest in Europe, yet we found it one of the most uncomfortable to play in. On the other hand, the Kongressaal in Vienna was a joy and reminded us very much of our own hall in Boston.

A good concert hall must have the quality of enveloping the listeners, yet not overpowering them, with sound. Unlike a theatre where the actors are detached from the audience, the concert hall must be constructed so that the music washes over the listener. He must become part of the performance, at least in a passive way.

Playing in the Boston Symphony Orchestra becomes, after a while, as it may or may not to members of other orchestras, a way of life. The rigorous schedule of daily rehearsals and concerts and the seasonal changes from the winter schedule to the spring Pops concerts, then to the outdoor Esplanade concerts, and finally to our summer Berkshire Festival season tend to make our lives almost completely dependent on the orchestra. Romances bloom within the family. Our former first cellist married the one lady cellist of the time; our assistant first violist married Fiedler's secretary; and fate had a hand in the marriage of Patsy Cardillo, our second clarinetist. We were on a midwinter orchestra tour and after the Saturday-night concert at Notre Dame University in South Bend we were in the small railroad station waiting for our train to take us to Chicago. It was a stormy, miserable night and the train was very late, so the orchestra "took over" the station. A few card games began on makeshift tables while in other areas of the station the usual clowning and horseplay took place. "Manny" Valerio, the smallest man in the orchestra, paraded around in the enormous coat of Ludwig Juht, one of the largest members of the orchestra. Because of the storm and the fact that nobody knew when the train would arrive, everyone stayed inside, and the reverberating noise in the station became almost unbearable. There were only a few local passengers and they seemed to be terrified by this band of lunatics. A very attractive young lady, sitting in a corner trying to read was constantly distracted by the shenanigans. Boaz Piller, one of our bassoonists, saw her, sat down next to her, and in his inimitable, charming, foreign-accented manner tried to console her. "Don't be 'fraid," he said. "Ve are all nice pipple." He then left her to seek out Pat Cardillo, one of the few young unmarried men of the orchestra. Pat was playing cards, but Piller tore him away from the game to meet the young lady. There was an introduction in which the name "Cardillo" was mentioned, but the girl's name was not. In fact, she refused to give it. After a few minutes of one-sided conversation the train finally arrived at about 2:30 A.M. The girl hurried into the public passenger cars while Pat joined the orchestra in the Boston Symphony cars. After the train had started and the inevitable poker game began, Patsy began to think about the beautiful, charming, frightened girl he had just met.

"What's her name?" asked Jimmy Stagliano, our first horn player.

"I don't know," answered Cardillo. "She wouldn't give it to me. I could get it if I wanted it." And he went back through the train looking for the young lady. About an hour later, after the train had stopped in La Porte, Indiana, where she got off, Patsy came back to the orchestra car, waving a piece of paper upon which was written not only the girl's name but her address and telephone number.

The girl from La Porte had spent the day shopping in South Bend, and had missed the earlier train back, which was why she had to wait for our train. And now, to condense in a few words the whirlwind courtship which followed, at first by mail, then by telephone, then by journeys to La Porte, they were married in the fall. Mr. and Mrs. Pasquale Cardillo now have four delightful children, three boys and a girl, of mixed Italian-Swedish, Midwestern-New England ancestry. All because of a missed train, a snowstorm, and a few other imponderables provided by fate and the tours of the Boston Symphony!

Tanglewood

The Berkshire Festival and Music Center at Tanglewood are a perpetual monument to Serge Koussevitzky. From the moment he saw for the first time the beautiful Berkshire Hills in western Massachusetts he began to imagine an artistic center and the fruition of a long-cherished dream. Actually the Berkshire Festival began a few years before Koussevitzky appeared on the scene. In the early thirties the American composer and conductor Henry Hadley had inaugurated a few weekend concerts with a group of musicians from the New York Philharmonic Orchestra, which were played under a tent on an estate near the present Tanglewood complex.

In 1936 Koussevitzky conducted the B.S.O. for the first time in the Berkshires and after two summers of concerts, some of which were disastrously rained out, the Tanglewood estate was given to the orchestra. A six-thousand-seat music shed was erected and in 1938 the vision of Koussevitzky began to take shape. He had imagined a school in which all the arts would be integrated—music, drama, painting, sculpture. One of his dreams was to revive Greek drama and to perform the works of all the great poets of the past.

Shortly after the erection of the music shed, a theatre-concert hall was built, and here were performed rare and unusual operas, and important premieres. The world premiere of Benjamin Britten's opera, "Peter Grimes" was but one of these and others were to follow.

In addition to the opera performances a series of chamber-music concerts, first by Boston Symphony members, then by world-famous chamber groups, began. The scope has steadily been enlarged until the present day when Tanglewood has become the scene of contemporary, avant-garde, experimental music and theatre, the kind which Bostonians are not yet ready for in their own city. If Koussey's dream of Greek drama has not been realized, that too will probably come in time.

The Berkshire Music Center has become an international eight-week summer school that attracts hundreds of young music students from many countries and trains them to take their place in the music profession as orchestral and chamber-music players, singers, and conductors. The roster of Tanglewood "alumni" is a long and illustrious one. In addition to the hundreds of players now in orchestras throughout this country and the world who have been students at Tanglewood, with a large proportion in our own Boston Symphony, the list includes Leonard Bernstein, Lukas Foss, Seiji Ozawa, Eleazar deCarvalho, and many others. Over the past twenty years many of the leading singers of the Metropolitan Opera have been Tanglewood alumni.

The Berkshire Music Center at Tanglewood is unique. No other orchestra has ever embarked upon the experiment of furthering the development of music and musicians, using its own players as faculty nucleus. The Boston Symphony was the pioneer in the idea of summer music festivals. Now other orchestras have followed suit, and it all must be attributed to Serge Koussevitzky.

Tanglewood has enhanced the lives of Boston Symphony players. There is, of course, the inevitable grumbling and complaining of some musicians, but for most of us it is a wonderful place to work and spend the summer. Many have either built or bought their own cottages, and with their families have become "Berkshirites."

Audiences at Tanglewood have changed over the years, and so has the tolerance of the management. In the early years people dressed formally, the ladies in evening dresses, the men in white or black jackets. Men were discouraged from attending without a tie and if an occasional lady showed up in shorts, she was given a wrap-around skirt to hide her legs. It is quite different today. Casual clothes are the rule and on a warm afternoon or evening the grass customers sometimes appear in bathing suits.

A large proportion of our Tanglewood audiences are not regular concert-goers, but they are much more enthusiastic than the usual musical sophisticates. They applaud loudly and

Tanglewood. Photograph by Whitestone Photo.

stormily before and after each performance. The long-established tradition of silence between movements of a symphony is consistently broken; and whereas the cautious, regular symphony-goer usually reserves his applause until he is sure a piece is over, our Tanglewood audiences constantly break in, sometimes even between cadences. Many patrons bring blankets and food and combine their picnics on the grass with a live Boston Symphony concert. Music for the masses has become a living reality at Tanglewood!

Youth Concerts at Symphony Hall

Unlike most symphony orchestras in the United States which devote a large part of their schedule to playing for young people, the Boston Symphony has, over the years, done very little in this field. There have been occasional special concerts for children. I remember attending one as a high school student with Serge Koussevitzky conducting and Wallace Goodrich of the New England Conservatory of Music commenting.

For some years the late Ernest Schelling presented a series of youth concerts in Jordan Hall, an auditorium about half the size of Symphony Hall, with an orchestra of Boston Symphony players. Later Wheeler Beckett presented for a few years an annual series of concerts in Symphony Hall with Boston Symphony personnel. These concerts were quite successful, yet for some reason they also came to an end; and for about a dozen years there were no young people's concerts in Symphony Hall.

In 1959 I decided to try to remedy what I considered a cultural lag in the lives of the young people of Greater Boston and to expose them to live music played by a great orchestra. With the help of a wonderful committee of dedicated people, sparked by the indomitable Bostonian Mrs. E. Anthony Kutten, we inaugurated the Youth Concerts at Symphony Hall, and our annual series of concerts have been sold out ever since.

It is not easy to organize thousands of youngsters into a symphony-going audience, regardless of the caliber of the concerts. It is a herculean job involving an enormous amount of detail and planning and were it not for our town-chairmen in each of some one hundred communities throughout Greater Boston who passionately believe in this kind of cultural, educational, and esthetic benefit to our young people and who handle myriad details, such as selling tickets and arranging transportation, plus the coordinating efforts of our quietly efficient and devoted secretary, Mrs. Manuel Kurland, these concerts would never have survived. Even the policemen who direct the traffic on Saturday mornings seem to like our concerts. Some of them occasionally come into the hall and, on one occasion, when we had a concert for handicapped children, an anonymous police captain supplied lollipops for more than two thousand youngsters.

Occasionally there arises the problem of a lost or strayed youngster. Long after the concert was ended on one wintry Saturday morning a little girl was found wandering outside the hall. A policeman brought her into the greenroom where some of the committee ladies and I were still discussing the concert. She told us her bus had left without her. "What happened?" I asked. "Oh," she answered, "I was walking to the bus with my school chums, but I stopped to talk to a dog." A telephone call was made to her home, which was quite a distance from Boston, and her father grudgingly came to get her.

Our programs are varied, and we have played music from the pre-baroque period to the ultra-modern, including an occasional avant-garde piece, which is much easier for a young person, without adult prejudices, to accept than his parents. We have even presented programs of jazz and music influenced by jazz, never attempting to influence the listener, but presenting all aspects of music and letting him make up his own mind.

If there is anything we have learned about young people it is that we must never play down to them. I am firmly convinced that there is no special music for the young. They can listen to all kinds, including some too "deep" for their elders. The only compromise one needs to make is to their listening attention span. In this regard I have tried to follow the advice of a psychologist who once told me that a child's listening span could be measured by his age. An eight-year-old could listen to an eight-minute piece, a ten-year-old to a ten-minute piece, etc.

Occasionally when trying to protect their sensibilities, we have been sharply rebuked. One Saturday morning we played Strauss' "Till Eulenspiegel," which I first explained with musical illustrations. When it came to the story of Till skipping merrily up the gallows (depicted by the saucy E-flat clarinet), I thought I would spare them and said, "And here Till skips up the steps of the gallows, and disappears into thin air. And for all we know he is still skipping around somewhere." A week later I got a letter from an irate nine-year-old boy. "That is wrong," he wrote. "He was hung!"

After a Youth Concert at Symphony Hall. Photograph by Photography Incorporated.

I get occasional letters from our young listeners and some of them display not only an interest in the music, but an unconscious humor. One boy of eleven wrote, "Dear Mr. Dickson: I enjoyed the concert very much. I have an ear for music and it listened to every bit."

Our final concert every year is our so-called "youth participation" program in which we present young high-school soloists who are chosen by competition and invite the Greater Boston Youth Symphony Orchestra, made up of high-school boys and girls, to join us of the Boston Symphony in a final selection. Each student sits next to a Boston Symphony player who takes the inside seat. At one concert we played the finale of Beethoven's Ninth Symphony with a chorus from four high schools and four student soloists from the New England Conservatory of Music.

We also present original compositions by high-school students. These students come from the neighboring town of Newton, where their teacher, Henry Lasker, a thoroughly trained professional composer and pianist, has demonstrated that young people can be taught to compose as well as to play. Their compositions are understandably derivative and imitative, but some show surprising originality. The mere fact that high-school students learn to compose and orchestrate their own works is, I think, remarkable; and to have their music played by a professional orchestra at a public concert gives these young people great incentive. Some of these fledgling composers have gone on to college to major in composition.

From time to time we present at our youth concerts father-and-son combinations when a Boston Symphony musician will play with his son, as, for instance, the Vivaldi Concerto for Two Bassoons played by Sherman Walt and his son Stephen; the Bach Double Violin Concerto played by George Zazofsky and his son Peter; or the Vivaldi Concerto for Two Trumpets played by Roger Voisin and his son Peter.

We have distinguished visitors at our youth concerts. Isaac Stern graciously appeared at our very first concert in 1959 and I remember how quietly interested the youngsters were, not only in his playing, but in his down-to-earth remarks and explanations. He asked how many played the violin, and after getting a show of hands, said, "It's tough to play the violin, isn't it? And you probably get discouraged as I did. But you must stick to it." And then he went on to explain how one must train himself, his hearing, his muscular co-ordination, etc. Then he played a G-major scale, slightly out of tune, and with a rather unpleasant, steely sound. "That is the way we all sound when we begin," he said, "but then with practice you develop your ear and control, and you begin to sound a little better." And he played the same G-major scale with such great beauty that the audience broke into wild applause. After that we played the finale of the Mendelssohn Concerto; first illustrating the themes, showing how the composer sometimes allows the orchestra to play the melody while the soloist accompanies it and, of course, vice versa; then the entire movement without pause. This humanistic approach to music, so charmingly carried out by Stern, is exactly what we have been striving for in all of our youth concerts.

From time to time I have introduced famous conductors to our young audiences. Charles Munch, Erich Leinsdorf, and Arthur Fiedler have all conducted segments of our programs. William Steinberg and Sir John Barbirolli have attended our concerts and were presented to the youngsters. An entire delegation of Russian composers, headed by Shostakovich and Kabalevsky, made their appearance one Saturday morning and after we played a piece by Shostakovich, I had the pleasure of introducing him from the stage.

Whether or not these concerts add to young people's "culture" (a word I abhor), they at least serve to introduce a certain amount of beauty into their young lives and will perhaps form the basis of a fuller and more enjoyable life. At least, we hope so.

The Pops and Esplanade Concerts

Back in the 1880's, a few years after Henry Lee Higginson established the Boston Symphony, he was made to realize that in order to keep his European musicians from deserting the orchestra he would have to provide them with more employment than that of the regular symphony season. He decided to add to the regular season a ten-week season of nightly light-music concerts, modeled somewhat after the London Prom concerts.

Since 1885 these popular concerts, now called Pops concerts, have become part and parcel of the spring tradition of the city of Boston. Other cities may have their symphony orchestras, but no other city in the United States has ever been able quite to duplicate the phenomenon of sold-out houses every night in the week for ten weeks, with a full symphony orchestra, without incurring a deficit. And the Boston Pops is not a separate organiza-

The author and Arthur Fiedler at a library conference. Photograph by Photography Incorporated.

tion from the Boston Symphony. With the exception of some first players the Pops personnel is substantially that of the Boston Symphony.

During the Pops season Symphony Hall is changed somewhat into a large beer-garden. The seats on the floor and indeed the floor itself are removed via a floor elevator that comes up from the basement at about the tenth row center. On the flat under floor are placed tables, four or five chairs to a table, all in rows, where the higher paying patrons listen to the music while sipping beer, wine, coffee, punch, and munching on nuts and sandwiches. There was a time when parties used to "visit" by pushing tables together and moving chairs in all directions, but since the

Coconut Grove fire in Boston fire laws demand that the tables be secured to the floor, and the chairs attached to them via chains.

The Pops has not always enjoyed its present popularity. There have been ups and downs. But when Arthur Fiedler took over in 1930 from the late Alfredo Casella and began to cater to public and current taste, the Pops assumed a popularity and success greater than ever before.

The success of the Pops, although vitally important to the over-all financial stability of the Boston Symphony, has not always sat well with certain B.S.O. conductors. Serge Koussevitzky particularly disliked the whole idea of his musicians "demeaning" themselves by playing arrangements of popular hits of the day. His prejudice was unfounded, for regardless of what music is played in the Pops there is always a striving for musical integrity on the part of conductor and player. And along with the popular music many major serious works have been first introduced by the Pops. over the past 40 years under Arthur Fiedler. It is the belief of many that the Pops have served their purpose faithfully by not only supplying good musical entertainment to the public, but by introducing many people who might otherwise have been immune to the beauty of music. Besides, the royalties from Pops recordings have played a substantial part in reducing the Boston Symphony's over-all deficit.

But in spite of these considerations, or perhaps because of them, we could always expect at our first rehearsal in Tanglewood, following the Pops season, a Koussevitzky tirade. After five minutes of rehearsing he would invariably stop and say, "Vot happened to mine orkester? I know! Too much Popst!"

If the regular symphony season is hard work, although always interesting, the Pops is more fun, although sometimes routinely boring. (It's awfully hard to keep interested, let alone be inspired, night after night.) But it is certain that we are more relaxed during the Pops season—especially each night during the latter part of the program when the "fun" pieces are introduced.

These include the current popular hits of the day, made into elaborate arrangements for a full symphony orchestra, mostly by the brilliant arranger Richard Hayman. Each season Arthur Fiedler orders these for the Pops and one or two become the season's favorites and are played almost every night. Some are occasionally played in subsequent seasons, but most become faded in a short time and are put away to gather dust on the attic-library shelves. One of these was an extremely raucous arrangement of the "Batman" theme, of TV fame, which we played for a few seasons. This required the rapid firing of a revolver during the closing measures, "played" by one of our percussion men, and it became customary at this point for our stage manager to launch from the stage ceiling a battalion of parachuted Batmen and a bagful of white goose feathers, all of which landed harmlessly among the musicians.

A number of years ago a Boston arranger, Peter Bodge, submitted to us a hilarious arrangement of Kincke's sugary "The Glowworm," which he titled "The Glowworm Turns." It was an immediate Pops "hit," and we still play it upon request. It requires among other effects fire gongs and an electric siren. One night when I was conducting and "The Glowworm Turns" had been requested, I was informed by our stage manager that the battery for the siren was dead. How could we play the piece without the siren? "Leave it to me," he said. "We'll fix it somehow." During the performance the siren worked perfectly, and it wasn't until long afterwards that I found out that the battery replacement was from my own car that was parked at the stage door!

One of the expected sounds during a Pops concert in Symphony Hall is that of the popping of champagne-bottle corks, a sound which varies in frequency from night to night. When the Christian Science people are present, there is no sound at all. On the other hand, during a Harvard night the sound reaches machine-gun proportions. Actually, the bottle-popping doesn't usually start until the latter part of the program. An occasional eager beaver in the audience, however, will begin celebrating at the beginning of the concert, much to the annoyance of Fiedler, who has instructed the champagne waiters to time their pops between numbers. A loud pop is particularly annoying during the playing of Handel's Largo. One evening there was a really loud blast during Pat Cardillo's clarinet cadenza in the "Orpheus" overture. Fiedler unconsciously ducked as though he had been shot, and Pat stood up while still playing, looked in the direction of the "shot" as though to say, "Leave the conductor alone. It's only me, and I'm doing the best I can!" and didn't miss a note. The popping of champagne corks has led to the belief that this was how the Pops got its name, but the truth is that nobody knows.

During my first Pops season I had as my stand partner Bernard Fiedler, Arthur's uncle. Benny, as we called him, was a real Fiedler in that he was a master of cynicism. At the first rehearsal he looked down on me and asked, "Why are you working so hard? That's not Koussevitzky. It's only Arthur!" Yet in spite of this seeming disregard for his nephew, he was proud of him and would have scratched your eyes out if you dared say anything against Arthur.

Benny's favorite pastime during a Pops concert was to greet old friends in the audience, even while the music was being played and he specifically ordered me to show him where we were should he get lost while greeting his friends. "Please," he said, "when I say 'Bixen, Bixen,' "—he never called anyone by his right name—"you should show me the place with your bow." Most of the music he knew by heart anyway, having played in the orchestra some forty-five years, but on occasion I was called upon to do some discreet bow pointing.

At one concert I got into serious trouble with Benny through no fault of my own. A lady pianist (who shall be nameless) was attempting to play the Franck Variations. Just as she began Benny noticed an old friend in the audience and while he was nodding to him, the pianist lost her memory and skipped about ten bars. The conductor valiantly tried to catch her, but as soon as he brought the orchestra up with her she immediately got lost again, and this game of cat and mouse went on during most of the performance. Benny kept shouting "Bixen, Bixen!" to me, but I was helpless and had to ignore him. I was having my own troubles trying to figure out where we were as were the rest of my colleagues. Benny took this as a personal insult and when the "performance" was finally over, he began to castigate me unmercifully. Until the day he died he held a grudge against me for not "showing me the place."

My own position in the Pops is a precarious one. Since 1955 I have been the assistant conductor of the Pops, but still play in the orchestra. This makes life a little difficult for me. On the days I am not conducting my colleagues look at me suspiciously and order me out of the musicians' tuning room. "This room is not for conductors!" they say. So I wander into Fiedler's room where he usually orders me out. "You're not conducting tonight. What are you doing here?" Once I asked him where I should go and he suggested the men's room. Of course this is all in fun—I hope—but some of my fellow players lead me to wonder, especially when someone plays a wrong note at rehearsal—even in the woodwinds—and everyone points at me. Once after a concert that I had conducted one of my fellow violinists said to me, "That was a great concert. The strings, especially, never sounded so good." I didn't quite know how to take it, until he followed it with "No wonder. You weren't playing!"

Another time after I had conducted a Pops concert our second bassoonist said to me on the following night, "Were you sick last night? I didn't see you."

"I was conducting," I said.

"Conducting? It seems to me if you were well enough to conduct, you were well enough to play!" And he walked away.

A word or two about "Mister Pops." Arthur Fiedler is one of the most remarkable men I have ever known and I have known him for many years. Since 1930 he has conducted the Boston Pops, far longer than any other conductor, and I daresay far longer than any conductor has ever conducted any orchestra anywhere in the world. Having started in the Boston Symphony as a violist in 1915, his association with the orchestra spans over fifty-three consecutive years. As a conductor of both serious and semiserious music, he has traveled to all parts of the world and to many music lovers his name is better known than that of any other conductor. Yet, in spite of his success, his attitude toward his work remains today that of a young man just starting on a career. Such is his peculiar and unique character that he does not even know that he is "the" Arthur Fiedler, or at least he has never paused to think about it. Each concert is, for him, a challenge, a step toward building a career.

Arthur Fiedler is and always has been a "loner." I have known him longer than have his wife and children and I think I am his friend, yet I don't think that I truly know him. There seems to be in his personality an inherent insulation that shuts out a really close relationship. There is about him something that does not allow for any sentiment or sentimentality and he accepts none from others. He has had some serious physical illnesses, but he has fought these with an amazing stoicism and he has won. One of Boston's leading heart specialists once told me that Arthur Fiedler has changed the thinking and prescribed treatment of doctors toward heart ailments, for Fiedler has steadfastly refused to follow their advice, and today, as he approaches his mid-seventies, he is vigorous, hale and hearty, and follows a schedule that would tax the energies of anyone half his age. Apart from his ten weeks of Boston Pops concerts he still travels constantly to the far corners of the globe, and for the past twenty years has conducted more concerts per year than any other conductor in the world. Last year alone he conducted almost two hundred concerts!

Back in 1929, one year before he became the conductor of the Pops, Arthur founded the Esplanade concerts, a series of outdoor summer concerts on the Charles River in downtown Boston, the first free symphony concerts to be given anywhere in the United States; these concerts have become the pattern for other such concerts throughout the country and they have become a summer habit for Boston. Each night, weather permitting, an average of fifteen thousand people come out to sit under the stars and listen to the music. If only for these concerts Arthur Fiedler has endeared himself to the people of Boston, and indeed they have named a bridge after him, a footbridge which spans Storrow

A morning Children's Concert at the Esplanade. Photograph by Photography Incorporated.

Drive and leads to the Esplanade. For the musicians these concerts are perhaps the most pleasant of all. There are, however, occasional hazards, all having to do with playing outdoors. We have been suddenly deluged by unpredictable New England rainstorms, in which case the concert has ended abruptly and unceremoniously as the musicians ran for cover like thieves, protecting their instruments.

Occasionally there is a bug invasion during a concert, when flying insects of enormous variety swarm into the shell, attacking the musicians and conductor indiscriminately. There was one occasion when a guest conductor tried to ward off one of these bugs and inadvertently brought the piece to a close two beats too early. One of our trumpeters almost choked on a bright green insect and became so nauseous he had to leave the stage. And my stand partner almost went out of his mind one night when a strange sound came out of his instrument even while he wasn't playing until he realized he was housing a large buzzing insect.

Another outdoor hazard is airplane noises. There is an understanding with the local airport that they will try to re-route planes so that they will not fly overhead during a concert, but an occasional music-loving pilot can't resist, especially during soft, slow movements—and sometimes we simply have to stop until he goes away. One night during an election campaign a blimp suddenly appeared overhead advertising John Volpe for Governor and Edward Brooke for Attorney-General. I wrote a scathing letter to both and got back a letter of apology. On another evening, while I was conducting the slow movement of a Beethoven symphony, the Goodyear blimp suddenly appeared overhead, quite low, motors whirling and flashing lights advertising Goodyear products. We stopped the concert, waited for the blimp to leave, then I went to the microphone and asked the huge audience not only to stop using whatever was being advertised, but to write to the company and protest this shameful display. The incident received national publicity, and the next day I had the uneasy feeling that perhaps I had done something wrong, but while I was waiting to be sued by the Goodyear Company, I received a telegram, then later a letter, of apology from the president of the company.

With few exceptions, each Pops night throughout the season is "sponsored" by various organizations, and their names appear on the program "among those present." These include women's clubs, fraternal groups, ethnic clubs, high-school and college groups, industrial organizations, and many others. Some nights are traditionally given over to only one group—like the Harvard twenty-fifth-reunion class, or the Tufts College graduating class, or the New England Conservatory, or the Eire Society, or the Israel Labor Organization. One of the most popular Pops evenings is the annual Old Timers' Night when the program is made up of old favorites and song medleys in which the audience is invited to sing along—and usually it does, with gusto.

The programs for the Pops are made with painstaking care about three weeks in advance. Those of us who are in on the program-making sessions know how fussy Fiedler is about each program and how constantly alert he is to the danger of routine. These sessions take place each week in the library, and they are attended by our two librarians, Fiedler's secretary, Fiedler, and myself. The requests of each organization are carefully considered, and, if possible, put into the program. If an unknown soloist has been requested by a particular group, he will be auditioned by Fiedler or me and, if he plays well, will be invited to appear with the orchestra. Many young aspiring soloists have thus received their first start with the Boston Pops.

The relationship of the Boston Pops to the Boston Symphony is a strange one. The Pops is tolerated as a kind of rich relative, coarse, unrefined, vulgar, but one who pays the bills and helps largely to support the whole family.

GUEST SOLOISTS

The loneliest and perhaps most pathetic figure in music is the traveling concert artist and why most young musicians aspire to be one is a mystery. True, the satisfaction of being applauded, sometimes adulated, for a good (or bad) performance cannot be explained to ordinary mortals, yet the cost to the performer is high. He travels from city to city with his accompanist or, if he is a pianist, by himself, hardly ever talking to anyone except "committee ladies" who invite him after the concert, when he is starved, to a reception with cookies and tea. It is no wonder that artists like Jascha Heifetz and Gregor Piatigorsky, after nearly a lifetime of such an existence, have suddenly said, "Enough!" and now limit their appearances to occasional gala concerts. I once asked Heifetz what he did while on tour. The answer I got was "I go to lots of burlesque shows and movies."

One day after a concert in which Piatigorsky was soloist with the Boston Symphony a small group of us were sitting in the greenroom chatting with him. Piatigorsky is one of the most charming, warmest, dearest human beings in the world, and he was expounding on his favorite topic—"giving up goddam cello!" All his life he has complained about his fate at having to face audiences whether he felt like it or not. And usually he has not! One of the great cellists of our time, he is also a witty raconteur and I have spent many hours listening to his fascinating stories. On this particular day he was complaining about nervousness before a concert.

"Grischa," I said, "you don't seem nervous at all when you come out."

"No?" he answered. "Before a concert I am shivering like baby. All the time—but especially in Boston."

"Well," I said, "you certainly know how to hide it. When you stride onto the stage you seem to exude nothing but confidence."

"I am a good actor," he said, "and, besides, lately I try psychology. Before concert I talk to myself. I say, 'Grischa, don't be nervous. You are the great Piatigorsky!' "

"Well," I asked, "does it help?"

"No," he said, "I don't believe myself!"

Jascha Heifetz is a legend in his own time. From time to time, since he does not perform very often these days, musicians will begin to have the suspicion that perhaps he is slipping just a little. Then he appears at a concert in Carnegie Hall and dazzles everyone into reaffirming that he is the greatest.

Once, I remember, he came out for rehearsal and turned to our first oboist, Fernand Gillet, for an "A." Gillet played it very pianissimo and Heifetz said to Koussevitzky, "Is he Scotch?" Koussevitzky, not understanding the humor at all, said, "No, he is French."

Gregor Piatigorsky by Olga Koussevitzky

Heifetz is an accomplished ping-pong player, having been at one time president of the American Ping-pong Association. I found out one evening that he hates to lose. Being the perfectionist he is, and having been accustomed his whole life to practicing that perfection, any effort on his part which does not represent his best, in no matter what category, seems to embarrass him. We were at the home of Joseph dePasquale, our first violist, who is no mean ping-pong player himself, and when he invited Heifetz to a game, Heifetz protested that he had not played for a long time and was out of practice. He consented to play, however, and although he did play quite well, he was soundly beaten by dePasquale. During the game he kept scolding himself and at the end was visibly upset.

Later in the evening we had tuned in the Louis-Marciano fight, which Louis lost, and Heifetz asked that the radio be turned off. "I don't like to witness the defeat of a great champion," he said.

It is not generally known that Heifetz is a good pianist; one night after dinner at Burgin's house he entertained us on the piano, playing musical puzzles, a game which he said was in vogue among his friends in California. He would play themes from the violin literature using the same notes the composer wrote, but disguised in different rhythms and with different note values and we had to guess what composition he was playing.

Heifetz's relationship with Richard Burgin was warm and mutually respectful. They had a high regard for one another and, I am told, when Heifetz became acquainted with the Sibelius Violin Concerto and then played it with astounding perfection, he first sought Burgin's musical advice. (Burgin had been among the first to introduce the work, in Finland in the presence of the composer.)

Concert artists generally add a touch of glamor to an orchestra and most orchestra players look forward to their appearance. There is always an electric atmosphere of expectation on the morning of the first rehearsal with a great soloist. A Rubinstein, a Heifetz, an Isaac Stern, each brings with him a personal kind of glamour and excitement. Each is far above the ordinary mortal.

Jascha Heifetz by Olga Koussevitzky

These are the people who bring zest to life and to living. What fun, for instance, when Artur Rubinstein appears at a rehearsal or recording session with us in the B.S.O.! Apart from his musical qualities, his charm, his wit, and his conversation attest to the perfectly civilized, cultured man. He has known, intimately, kings and queens and Presidents and dictators, all of whom have sought out his company. Yet, with all his fame and glory Rubinstein remains a modest man, almost self-deprecating. Once at a recording session after the first "take" of the Tchaikovsky Concerto he said, "I played enough wrong notes to write a whole new concerto. Now let us do it again!" I remember that recording session vividly, for each playback was better than the previous one until, after five hours—at one o'clock in the morning—Rubinstein said, "Now I could begin all over again." He was then eighty! But we did not do it over again. The rest of us were too tired. Later Rubinstein said, "I don't know why they ask me to record. The young crop of pianists play rings around me." And then he added, "Well, perhaps I am still a better musician, eh?"

Perhaps the most energetic of all concert artists is the violinist Isaac Stern. He plays more concerts per year than any other artist and, in addition, finds time to engage in humanitarian and civic pursuits. He is extremely articulate as a speaker, writer, and raconteur. Stern is responsible, almost singlehandedly, for the preservation of Carnegie Hall, which, but for his efforts, would now be the site of an office building or parking lot. At rehearsals Stern is the most easy-going of all violinists. He genuinely enjoys what he is doing and seems to invite the orchestra to make music with him. His camaraderie with the musicians is quite a contrast to Heifetz's aloofness. Yet, for some strange reason, musicians in the orchestra resent Stern's friendly approach. One of our clarinetists was highly insulted because Stern dared to make a direct musical suggestion to him, instead of transmitting his wishes through the conductor (the accepted procedure for the soloist). When Stern rehearses he is apt to approach each section of the orchestra, making comments and suggestions while he is playing. As for myself, I rather like this way of making music. I think it saves time. It certainly is not intended, on Stern's part, to be anything but a means to a better performance.

Artur Rubinstein by Olga Koussevitzky

I suppose Isaac practices or has practiced a great deal, but *when* is a great mystery, for he is constantly engaged in some activity outside of music. Being one of the most naturally gifted violinists I have ever known, he must rely to a very great degree on his talent. I remember a number of years ago when he was giving a recital in Symphony Hall on a Sunday afternoon and had asked if I would turn pages for his pianist. It was a cold, wintry day in January, the concert was scheduled for 3:30 P.M., and at exactly 3:25 Stern arrived, told me he hadn't touched the violin since Friday, took it out of the case, scratched out a few notes, was told by the frantic manager that it was time to begin, walked out calmly onto the stage, and played an absolutely gorgeous performance of the Handel D Major Sonata. By this time he was sufficiently warmed up to continue with a two-hour display of technical and musical wizardry.

The great Soviet violinist David Oistrakh first came to the United States in 1955, and following a sensational debut in Carnegie Hall on Sunday evening, November twentieth, came to Boston shortly thereafter to play with us. While he was in Boston, I think I helped avert, with the help of Richard Burgin, our concertmaster, an international incident. But before I get to that let me first describe that Carnegie Hall concert, which I was fortunate enough to attend. Oistrakh was known to the American public only through his recordings, and these were enough to stimulate interest among musicians. In addition, there was the fact that until then no Soviet artist had been allowed to come to the United States and here was a live curiosity. Carnegie Hall was packed for the occasion and it seemed that every fiddler in the world was there. His reception from the start was warm, friendly, exciting, and with each piece he played the excitement grew in intensity and at the end of the concert the audience went wild.

The only one who seemed unimpressed as I watched him was Mischa Elman, and I kept thinking of the legendary story of Jascha Heifetz's debut in the same hall many years earlier when Elman, who was sitting with the pianist Leopold Godowsky, turned to him during the intermission and said, "Awfully hot here," and Godowsky replied, "Not for pianists!" At the Oistrakh concert during the intermission, while the audience stood and shouted, Elman calmly walked up the aisle looking terribly unconcerned; and it is said that he complained to a friend, "I don't know why they make such a fuss. Even Heifetz plays better!"

After the concert I somehow made my way to Oistrakh's room and when I asked him why he had not included Boston in his tour of the United States, he told me that he had not been invited, but would consider it a great privilege to play with the Boston Symphony. I told him that he would hear from us (I had absolutely no authority!) and when I returned to Boston the next day I immediately informed our management that Oistrakh was available and eager, whereupon the machinery was set in motion for him to play in Symphony Hall with us at a special pension fund concert and to make recordings a few weeks later.

On the day Oistrakh arrived in Boston I was given the assignment of calling for him at his hotel and bringing him to Symphony Hall. R.C.A. Victor had already installed their microphones, machines, etc., in the hall, and Munch and the musicians were ready to start the recording session with Oistrakh. I showed him to the greenroom where he took out his violin and began to warm up. It was at this precise moment that Thomas Perry, the manager, received a phone call from Petrillo's office in Chicago with the information that since Oistrakh was not a member of the musicians' union and since no permission had been asked by him or his manager, he would not be allowed to record with us. Our manager rushed down to the greenroom where he fortunately found Burgin, our concertmaster, busily engaged in Russian conversation with Oistrakh. He took Burgin aside and told him what had happened and asked him to explain to Oistrakh that he would try to resolve the situation. Then Burgin went back to the stage where the orchestra was preparing to record an orchestral piece while Perry went back to the phone and I was asked to stay with Oistrakh.

He practiced for a while, then suddenly said, "Please take me back to the hotel," and began to put away his violin. I pleaded with him to stay, but he was adamant. "No," he said in German, "if they don't want me, I will not stay." I rushed out for Burgin, who came into the room and in his gentle, persuasive way explained that it was all a misunderstanding, and that in a few minutes everything would be resolved. At one point Oistrakh turned to me and uttered what seemed a classic statement. "In my country," he said, "we do not have this. No one tells me what to do!" In a few minutes Perry reappeared to inform Oistrakh that permission had been granted; and he walked onto the stage to a thunderous ovation from the orchestra.

Since the trail-blazing visit of Oistrakh a number of Soviet artists have come to the United States and most have appeared with the Boston Symphony. The fine violinist, Leonid Kogan, made his American debut with us in 1958. Like other Russians, Kogan seemed noncommittal about the United States. I never heard him praise anything. And one night while I was driving him to a party, he asked if he could drive my car. I let him take the wheel only to discover that he drove like a lunatic. He drove so fast through the streets of Boston that I thought certainly we would be stopped by a policeman. I'm not sure that I even had the right to allow my car to be driven by a foreigner. When we arrived, he said, "You have good car, but mine is better." I asked him what kind of a car he had, expecting to hear the name of a Russian-built automobile. "I have Buick Special!" he said proudly.

As in any other business or profession there are rivalries in the music business, too, especially among concert artists, and most of these "feuds" grow until they become legends. There was the celebrated rivalry between Koussevitzky and Toscanini. Neither was ever allowed to conduct the other's orchestra. Statements have been attributed to each about the other, yet who is there to swear to them? Koussevitzky is supposed to have said, when asked about Toscanini, "Very good for Italian opera"; and Toscanini is supposed to have retorted, "Such a bad conductor, and the orchestra plays so well!"

One of the most legendary rivalries was that between Elman and Heifetz. I once said to Heifetz at a party, "You must hear an awful lot of stories about yourself," and he answered, "No, strangely enough all the stories I hear are about Elman!" Elman came to the United States long before Heifetz and was well established here when Heifetz made his memorable Carnegie Hall debut at the age of sixteen; and that was when all the stories began. Once, when Mrs. Elman was wheeling her infant son through Central Park a neighbor who knew only that the baby's father played the violin stopped to admire the child. "Will he be a violinist?" she asked.

"I hope so," replied Mrs. Elman.

Whereupon the neighbor said, "Maybe another Heifetz?" And Mrs. Elman turned away huffily.

Vladimir Resnikoff, retired member of the Boston Symphony, was a close friend of Elman and he tells of the time when Elman arrived in San Francisco for a concert and on the way to his hotel decided to stop and visit a great-aunt. Knowing how much she loved his playing, especially of the Schubert "Ave Maria," he stopped at a record shop intending to buy his own recording for her. He approached the clerk and asked for the record. The clerk went into the back room, soon came back, and announced, "I'm sorry we're all out of the Elman recording, but we have a much better one by Heifetz." Elman thanked him and left, of course without buying it. Later when he recounted the incident to Resnikoff, he said, "I felt very bad when he told me the Heifetz one was better, but then I said to myself, 'Don't feel so bad. Your record is all sold out! Heifetz's they have plenty! So whose is better?' "

Jascha Heifetz once ridiculed the term "delicate concert artist" when he decided that fifty years on the concert stage was enough. "The 'delicate concert artist,' " he said, "must have the nerves of a bull-fighter, the digestion of a peasant, the hide of a politician, and the tact of a night-club hostess." One who gives the appearance of the "delicate artist" is the world-renowned violinist, Yehudi Menuhin. Yet he is anything but. A practitioner of Yoga, he keeps himself in fine physical and mental condition. Once at a rehearsal with us he put down his violin, stood on his head for a few minutes, then resumed playing!

Menuhin has had a fantastic career. Starting as one of the most astounding prodigies the world has ever known, he gave his first public concert at the age of seven with the San Francisco Symphony and has been playing publicly ever since. In his twenties he went into temporary retirement for further study and self-evaluation and there are those who maintain that his playing then began to deteriorate. He remains, however, a great artist, teacher, and musician, contributing much to the culture of the world.

Once at a concert with us in Paris Menuhin was so carried away with the tremendous ovation he received from the audience that he came out and played an unaccompanied encore (the

Bach E Major Prelude), and so infuriated our manager that for many years he was not invited to play with us.

During the twenties and thirties the names of Fritz Kreisler, Mischa Elman, and Jascha Heifetz dominated the field of violinists and there is an apocryphal story that Elman and Heifetz were having lunch together when the headwaiter brought an envelope to their table, addressed to "the world's greatest violinist." Heifetz read the envelope and said, "This is for you, Mischa."

Elman took it, read it, and handed it back. "No, it is for you, Jascha," he insisted.

"Well," said Heifetz as he passed back the envelope, "open it anyway." Elman did, and his face fell. "What does it say, Mischa?" Heifetz asked.

"It says," replied Elman, "Dear Fritz!"

The late Fritz Kreisler was once engaged by a society matron to play for her friends at a soiree at her home. Kreisler told her that his fee would be one thousand dollars. She agreed and then added, "You will not mingle with my guests." Whereupon Kreisler said, "In that case my fee will be only five hundred dollars."

In the early history of the Boston Symphony very few lady cellists appeared as soloists. The unwieldy instrument was perhaps considered too difficult for the weaker sex and there was a time when it was even considered unladylike to play an instrument that had to be straddled. Indeed some of the early lady cellists actually played the instrument sidesaddle! One of the pioneers of the cello was the great English cellist, Beatrice Harrison, who, with her protective flowing skirt, dared to play her instrument in front of her and whose greatest compliment from the press and fellow musicians was that she played like a man.

In the thirties there appeared on the American concert scene the diminutive Russian cellist, Raya Garbousova. She was a great favorite of Koussevitzky and appeared with us a number of times. Once during a rehearsal of the Haydn Concerto she stopped and said to Koussevitzky, "Serge Alexandrovitch, the orchestra is too loud. I cannot hear myself!"

To which Koussevitzky replied, "You must play louder!"

"But I am playing as loud as I can!" she answered.

"Then," said Koussevitzky, "you must eat more 'kasha!' "

Accidents sometimes occur during performances which add to the over-all excitement. Strings snap, bows break, pianos collapse, all during performances when least expected. The most common minor catastrophe is the sudden popping of a violin or cello string. When it happens to a player in the orchestra, he merely stops playing and puts on a fresh string while the others carry on. Some of us who never carry extra strings rely on those who do and when the inevitable happens, we look frantically at our favorite benefactor who, seeing our plight, stops playing at the next three- or four-bar rest, and hands us his trusty string pouch.

If a violin soloist should break a string during a performance, he quickly exchanges instruments with the concertmaster, who hands it to the assistant concertmaster in exchange for his violin, and the assistant concertmaster replaces the broken string. Sometimes this all is done so quickly and expertly that only those in the front rows are aware of what has happened. Once we witnessed a startling accident to Ruggiero Ricci, when his bow actually broke during a televised concert from Sanders Theatre in Cambridge. He was playing the last movement of the Sibelius Violin Concerto, sawing away furiously when the bow snapped with a loud crack. For a moment his violin and fingers became entangled in horse hair, but he nonchalantly dropped the wounded stick, reached out to our concertmaster's already outstretched arm, took his bow and continued to the end of the piece, having missed about two bars of music.

At a Symphony Hall concert with Rudolf Serkin as soloist in the Brahms Second Piano Concerto during the slow movement the loud pedal suddenly collapsed. (Anyone who has seen Serkin attack a piano might wonder why this does not happen more often!) He stopped, left the stage, and went looking for the Steinway piano tuner, Zeke Walker, who was sitting backstage, and brought him to the sick piano. Walker assessed the situation, called for a crowbar and hammer, and went to work. After a few minutes on his hands and knees he had the pedal repaired and received a standing ovation from the audience, who, I am sure, had never before witnessed the repairing of a piano during a concert by a blind man!

Some of us in the orchestra remember the late great pianist Josef Hofmann. He had had a fabulous career as a giant of a pianist, as director of the Curtis Institute in Philadelphia, and, surprisingly, as an inventor of mechanical gadgets from which he made a lot of money.

Hofmann was a curmudgeon of a man, who seemed to hate everybody, but mostly conductors. His favorite pastime when playing with an orchestra was to try to throw the conductor and he would employ all kinds of irritating devices to accomplish his purpose, like taking impossibly fast tempos, sudden rubatos, illogical changes of tempo and dynamics. I remember a performance of the Schumann Piano Concerto with Koussevitzky in which the orchestra was hardly ever together with the soloist. Everything would go along beautifully for a few bars and then suddenly Hofmann would change the tempo, causing Koussevitzky to start waving frantically at the orchestra; and no sooner were we on the track than he would go off again. All the time there was a devilish look of supreme satisfaction on his face. Hofmann once told Richard Burgin that the only conductor he was never able to lose was Karl Muck.

The late Artur Schnabel last played with the Boston Symphony during a Beethoven festival in 1936 (two years before I joined the orchestra) and I am told there were also some personality clashes between him and Koussevitzky. Both men had iron wills, both had enormous egos, and endless discussions and arguments took place during rehearsal. Schnabel was a highly cultured musician and a so-called Beethoven "expert." He was also conceited and tactless and was used to having things his way and Koussevitzky was equally conceited, if perhaps slightly less cerebral in his approach to Beethoven. I am told those rehearsals were filled with fireworks. After one of the performances someone asked Schnabel if Koussevitzky followed him well, and Schnabel acidly replied, "He follows only too well. I wish he were *with* me more!"

A soloist usually rehearses once, almost always at the last rehearsal of the week. If he is playing a standard work, the rehearsal is generally a perfunctory one in which there are few stops or corrections. It is merely to acquaint or re-acquaint the soloist with the orchestra, conductor, and the acoustics of the hall.

If the work is a new one, the soloist often comes a day or two earlier and there are more rehearsals. For the Barber Piano Concerto, commissioned for the opening of Lincoln Center, John Browning, the pianist, worked with us for a whole week before the premiere performance in New York.

In the old days soloists would often not rehearse at all. Jacques Thibaud, the suave French violinist, once came to play the Beethoven Concerto and, of course, he did not rehearse, since he had played it with us many times. He arrived at Symphony Hall the day of the concert only a few minutes before he had to play, grabbed his violin and walked out on the stage to play the Beethoven Violin Concerto.

At least he *thought* he was going to play the Beethoven Violin Concerto and he rather looked forward to the long introduction by the orchestra, which would give him time to compose himself, and catch his breath. However, the program read Mendelssohn Violin Concerto and, as everybody knows, this concerto has practically no introduction. The orchestra plays one and a half bars and the soloist begins.

After Thibaud tuned his violin he nodded to the conductor and put his violin by his side. The conductor, eyeing him quizzically, couldn't understand why the violin wasn't at his chin, ready to play, and Thibaud couldn't understand why the conductor didn't get on with the piece. After a number of nods and bows to one another the conductor simply began. And Thibaud almost decapitated himself as he swung his violin up to his chin! "Why didn't you tell me it was Mendelssohn?" he asked. Back came the reply: "Why didn't you ask me?" And there followed a flawless performance.

Egon Petri, the late Dutch pianist, once told me of a performance of the Beethoven Fourth Piano Concerto in which he forgot the very beginning! It begins with the piano playing alone for four bars, but at rehearsal Petri would dispense with his opening solo. The orchestra would begin after the four measures, play its long introduction, then he would join them. At the concert Petri completely forgot that he had to start the piece. He nodded to the conductor, the conductor nodded back, he nodded again, the conductor nodded again, and this went on for quite a while. Until Petri suddenly realized that *he* had to begin. It was then that his mind went completely blank and he couldn't remember how. He got up from the piano, walked over to the podium, glanced at the score, then went back to his seat, and started.

THOUGHTS ABOUT MUSIC CRITICS

We musicians play a great number of concerts every year, yet no concert ever seems to be routine. Surely there are nights when we fall short of the mark, and who can explain the chemistry of what makes a concert start off and continue to get better and better with each movement or each composition? Or the opposite, when nothing seems to be right, when the evil spirits are plaguing our fingers and embouchures, and the beat of the tympani feels like a jabbing pain in our sinuses, and the conductor seems to be completely aloof from the orchestra, and the audience seems completely hostile. After such concerts we sneak back to our domiciles, snap at our wives, and go to bed. Then, the next morning we read a glowing account of a wonderful performance, written by an erudite music critic, and we shrug our shoulders. We also shrug our shoulders when we receive a bad notice of a good concert.

Music critics are an *un*necessary evil. They serve no useful purpose and, fortunately, have had no effect whatsoever upon the course of musical history. Many of them don't know anything about music and those who know a great deal about it have no feeling for it. They go to concerts to criticize, not to enjoy. Too many of us are influenced by their opinions and their opinions have been proved notably wrong throughout history. If critics had been right, we would have no Beethoven or Brahms or Schubert.

Music is like food. Everyone can enjoy it and, like food, it can sometimes be distasteful, sometimes delightful; but no one needs a critic to tell him how good or bad it is. A musical gourmet develops his own sense of taste.

Critics can be confusing to the average listener. After a performance of Alban Berg's opera "Lulu" a lady called me the next morning and said, "I have been reading in the paper that it was written in the twelve-tone row. No wonder I didn't enjoy it. I was in the sixteenth row!"

Some critics of the past have engaged in harsh invective, but at least it had the questionable virtue of being cruelly humorous. A Viennese critic once wrote about a violinist, Professor Green, as follows: "Green is good for the eyes but not for the ears." After another concert by a well-known singer he wrote, "If she had in her high register what she lacks in her low register, her middle register would not be so intolerable!"

And in this country a critic once wrote, "Mr. —— played last night in the Hollywood Bowl. They should have flushed it."

Most musicians harbor the secret ambition of somehow getting back at the critic and one did in his own way. The German composer-pianist, Max Reger, on receiving a bad review, wrote to the critic: "Dear Sir, I am in the smallest room of my house with your criticism before me. In a moment it will be behind me! Your obedient servant, Max Reger."

Pierre Monteux once said to a group of newspapermen, "I started my career as a violinist. When that became too difficult, I became a viola player. When that became too difficult, I became a conductor. And when I can no longer do anything, I will become a critic."

Lest I seem unduly bitter, let me say that I have enjoyed the friendship of some critics, have admired their musical knowledge, and have even learned from them. In person they are most charming. It is only when they sit down to write that they become fiends.

One of the most erudite critics in Boston is Michael Steinberg, a man whom, strangely enough, I consider a friend. When Michael came to Boston a few years ago to replace the late Cyrus Durgin as music editor of *The Boston Globe* he immediately became controversial and he has remained so. People now buy the *Globe* to see how vitriolic Steinberg can be about a performance, especially by the Boston Symphony. When he was once asked why he found it necessary to be so vicious, he replied, "Music critics are supposed to be policemen of the musical standards of a community, and sheep make bad policemen." "Agreed," I said, "but do tigers make better policemen?" He smiled solicitously.

OUR FAITHFUL SUBSCRIBERS

From the stage of Symphony Hall, as we look out into the audience, the faces of our faithful listeners have become, over the years, as familiar to us as ours to them. Indeed, if the "big hat" isn't in her usual seat on Friday afternoon my partner and I are a bit concerned and look for her eagerly on the following Friday.

Our oldest regular audience is that of Friday afternoon. For this series it is practically impossible to buy tickets. They have been held in the same family for generations and are handed down from father to son, mother to daughter. And going to the Friday-afternoon symphony is a religious ritual for all proper Bostonians.

One problem with the Friday-afternoon audiences has never quite been solved, that of early-leavers. Unlike the distracting habit of opera-goers who habitually miss the first act of every opera, there are a number of Friday-afternoon listeners who have never heard the last movement of most symphonies. No matter how short the concert is, or how early the time, as soon as the next-to-last movement is over, there is a determined rush for the exit; and some of the ladies are so expert at timing that they are able to make the door just before the last movement begins. We have already moved up our concert starting time from 2:30 to 2:00, but this has had no discernible effect upon the pathological early-risers. I wonder if it wouldn't be a good idea to give a series of concerts of only last movements, in order to acquaint our customers with what they have been missing all these years. Or, perhaps we should begin symphonies with the last movement.

There is an apocryphal story about an elderly couple and their son who occupied the same seats for years. One Friday afternoon the lady occupied her usual seat, but the two seats beside her were vacant. During the intermission she was asked by a friend why she was alone. "Oh," she said, "my husband passed away."

"And where is your son?" she was asked.

"Well," she replied, "someone had to go to the funeral."

Our Friday-afternoon audiences are not inherently boisterous, and sometimes the native reserve of these Back Bay ladies, plus the fact that they are not overly strong to begin with, creates embarrassing situations at the end of a concert, especially when their applause dies down before the conductor or soloist has had time to walk off the stage. Often we musicians can see them applauding, but can't hear them and sometimes I am tempted to run after the soloist and say, "Please come back for a bow. They really like you!" After one of these concerts Jascha Heifetz once said to me, "These Friday-afternoon concerts would be so much more enjoyable if the ladies would only remove their gloves."

The only time I ever saw the Friday audience in an uproar was when Vladimir Horowitz made his debut with the Boston Symphony. At that concert the ladies not only removed their gloves, but resorted to pounding their canes on the floor!

Yes, this is a discriminating audience which, after many years of concert-going, is much less conservative than one would imagine. I have heard heated discussions in the corridors of Symphony Hall by elderly ladies in defense of the music of Bartók and Schoenberg and Webern. (Alas, I have also heard some strange remarks before concerts, like the following: "Agatha, what are they playing today?" "Brahms' Fourth in E Minor." "Oh, I hate minor symphonies, don't you?")

Our Saturday-night audience, second in age and prestige, is quite different from Friday's. It is more earthy, more outspoken, and more bourgeois in its attitude and behavior. It is also not as loyal. One constantly sees new faces (not new subscribers!)—who have been given or sold tickets for a concert that didn't appeal to the regular ticket-holder. This audience is the fussiest of all. They constantly write letters complaining about the programs, especially about "too much modern music." Without a moment's hesitation they will leap from their seats at the conclusion of a new work with which they are completely unfamiliar, even after hearing it, and hasten to deliver to one of us in the corridor an erudite musical denunciation.

My fourth-desk partner, with whom I have been sitting for many years, loves to scan the audience before a concert. He usually comes out a few minutes early and when I have arrived, he files an oral report on where the pretty girls are sitting. For a few years he and I witnessed a real-life cycle take place before our eyes. Each Saturday night a young man would dash in at the last minute before the conductor came on the stage and breathlessly take his seat in the first row just below us, and each week he had with him a different girl, equally breathless as she sat down next to him. We used to watch this man explain the music to his friend after each movement and during the music he would quietly conduct along, sway with the music, and occasionally look knowingly at the girl. I must say the girls seemed very impressed. The young man would also greet us with an approving nod after a piece was finished and the fact that he knew us also seemed to impress the girls. Each week my partner and I would conjecture as to what kind she would be—blonde, brunette, redhead?

Then we suddenly noticed that there was no more variety. The same girl was there with him week after week. We noticed a diamond ring on her left hand and at the same time the young man discontinued his swaying and conducting. At the very first concert of the following season we eagerly awaited our young couple and, sure enough, they both came in, early, and greeted us warmly. This time I noticed, during the overture to "The Marriage of Figaro," that they both wore wedding rings.

After a few months my colleague, who has five children and knows about these things, whispered to me, "She's pregnant." And week after week there was more and more tangible evidence that my colleague was right. Then for a few weeks before the close of that season we noticed different people in those front-row seats. And at the final concert of the season, while we were already seated on the stage, in walked our young couple, she quite thin again. He came directly to the stage, took out two cigars, and handed them to us. "A boy!" he said.

If the Friday audience is different from the Saturday audience, the Tuesday audience is different from both, and the brand new Thursday audience is the most different of all. Let us first consider the Tuesday-night audience, which is divided into two series, the old Harvard University Sanders Theatre concerts now transplanted to Symphony Hall, and the newer Tuesday-night series. The former audience is still largely college people—faculty and their families, former teachers and students—also Dr. and Mrs. Paul Dudley White. The other Tuesday series seems to be made up largely of very appreciative, good-listening professional people—doctors, lawyers, etc.

Of all our formal audiences the newest is usually the most enthusiastic and our newest audience today is the Thursday audience. But our most vital, live, and swinging audience is our informal "open rehearsal" audience, who come on eight Thursday nights. These audiences are mainly college and high-school youngsters and they are knowledgeable, bright, and enthusiastic.

Even our out-of-town listeners in New York and Providence have become familiar to us and each year, at the opening concert, we are in the habit of greeting old friends from the stage. There is, however, one "old friend" in the front row at our Providence concerts whom we try to avoid. He is quite evidently a would-be conductor, perhaps a bit frustrated, who comes to the concert armed with scores and conducts the entire program from his seat. The reason we try to avoid him is that his "beat" is rather unorthodox and he is apt to confuse us if we should inadvertently look at him. I remember playing a Tchaikovsky symphony in which Charles Munch had made a couple of substantial cuts, and at the Providence performance I watched our friend. When we made the first cut he kept on blithely conducting for many bars until he suddenly realized something was wrong. He began to turn pages back and forth furiously. And just as he found the place, we made another cut. This time he just couldn't keep up with the orchestra and when we finished the movement, he was still turning pages, and perspiring profusely.

THE NEXT THIRTY YEARS

And now what of the future of the Boston Symphony?

The next thirty years will probably bring about drastic changes in style, in taste, and even in personnel. Important musicians like Leonard Bernstein, Lukas Foss, and others have already stated that the symphony orchestra as such will soon be relegated to the status of a museum, that the music of the future will not be confined to performance by an orchestra with the standardized and prescribed instrumental formulas of today. Not necessarily will the composer of tomorrow have in mind eighteen first violins, sixteen second violins, twelve violas, twelve cellos, and ten basses, plus a certain number of woodwinds, brasses, and percussion instruments. He may have an entirely different conception of sound, as indeed do many of our avant-garde composers of today, a sound that is produced by entirely different kinds of in-

Opposite: A future B.S.O. rehearsal? Photograph by Robert Berkovitz.

struments. In the electronic future music may be entirely computerized, and musical instruments as we know them may be discarded in favor of electronic machines. Perhaps the concert-goer of tomorrow will come to Symphony Hall, adjust his Martian headpiece, and "tune in" to a concert played by an "orchestra" of seventeen boxes and four engineers. If he removes his headset, he will miss some of the sounds inaudible to the human ear; also, the loudest music would shatter his eardrums. The "conductor" will not be seen. He will be in a soundproof compartment at the rear of the hall, high above the second balcony, where he will relay his pre-rehearsed directions to his colleagues on the stage; and after the concert he will slide down in a suspended gondola to take his bows.

By the year 2000 all of us will probably have become so sophisticated and so saturated with music that all emotion will have been drained out of our systems. Concert-going will be an exercise in brain-function, nothing more. Perhaps it will afford a kind of satisfaction we don't quite understand today, but I'm glad I won't be around to "enjoy" it.